# THE GAME
# I LOVE

*Wisdom, Insight, and*
*Instruction from*
*Golf's Greatest Player*

# SAM SNEAD
## *with Fran Pirozzolo*

Published by Random House Large Print
in association with Ballantine Books
New York 1997

*Library of Congress Cataloging-in-Publication Data*
Snead, Sam, 1912–
The game I love : wisdom, insight, and instruction from
golf's greatest player / Sam Snead with Fran Pirozzolo.
p. cm.
ISBN 0-679-77428-9
1. Golf—Study and teaching. 2. Golf—Anecdotes.
3. Snead, Sam, 1912– . 4. Large type books.
I. Pirozzolo, Francis J. II. Title.
GV965.S658  1997
796.352—dc21                                  96-48649
                                                  CIP

Random House Web Address: http://www.randomhouse.com/
*Printed in the United States of America*
FIRST LARGE PRINT EDITION

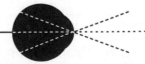

This Large Print Book carries the
Seal of Approval of N.A.V.H.

# CONTENTS

| | |
|---|---|
| ACKNOWLEDGMENTS | XI |
| Introduction and Swing Diagnosis *by Jim McLean* | XIII |
| Greetings from Sam | XIX |
| My First Day in Golf | 1 |
| Learning to Swing a Club | 2 |
| Advice to Parents | 3 |
| Stick with the Basics | 5 |
| *Fran Pirozzolo on Simplicity* | 6 |
| Music and Swing Tempo | 8 |
| *Tom Watson on Sam's Rhythm* | 9 |
| The First Match | 10 |
| Harold Bell | 11 |
| The Importance of Physical Conditioning | 13 |
| Lessons of the Hickory Stick | 14 |
| The Changeover | 15 |
| Goals | 16 |
| Being Surrounded by Others Who Believe in You | 18 |
| Strings and Stones | 20 |
| Deprivation as a Competitive Advantage | 22 |
| Extraordinary Experiences | 23 |
| The First Lesson | 25 |

Advice to Teachers of the Game                     26
Covering the Strike Zone                           29
The Cascades Open—1935                             30
The Grip                                           32
Never Give Up—Never Give In                        34
Giving Up                                          36
The Original Big Bertha                            37
For Extra Distance                                 39
More Thoughts About the Grip                       40
Bobby Jones                                        42
Best Dressed and Well Fed                          44
Grip Pressure                                      46
Company Man                                        47
Gaining an Edge                                    48
*Judy Rankin on the One-Piece Takeaway*            50
The Athletic Start-up to the Swing                 52
The Ryder Cup                                      53
The Plane Truth                                    55
The 1938 PGA: I Get a Short-Game Lesson            56
The Wedge                                          58
*Dick Harmon on Sam's Wedge Play*                  59
Lighthorse Harry Cooper                            60
Life on the Road                                   62
The Snead Squat                                    63
We Played to Have Fun, Too                         65
The Most Important Clubs                           68
Henry Picard Picks Me Up                           70
Alignment for Intentional Hooks and Slices         71
A Feel for the Club Face                           73
Life with Audrey                                   74
Bunker Play                                        76
The 1942 PGA Championship                          78

My Take on the Driver Swing                            81
Visualization and Mental Rehearsal                     83
The 1946 British Open                                  84
Blueprinting                                           87
Mental Maturity                                        90
Diegeling with Leo                                     91
The Relaxation Response                                94
The Killer Instinct                                    95
Jimmy Demaret                                          97
Breathing and Heart Rate                               99
*Byron Nelson on Sam*                                 100
Lord Byron                                            102
In the Zone                                           107
Bantam Ben Hogan                                      110
Ben Hogan, Byron Nelson, and Me                       113
Concentration: The Key to Success                     118
Beating Hogan at Riviera                              119
1950: Sweet and Bitter                                122
Playing from the Ground Up                            124
Masters Memories                                      126
The 1954 Masters                                      127
Left Holding the Bag                                  132
Tour School—The Old Days                              134
The Best Putter I Ever Saw                            136
Obstacles to Performance                              138
U.S. Opens Lost                                       139
Coping with Defeat                                    144
More on Predestination                                148
Staying Hot While Keeping Cool                        150
Get a Grip                                            153
If You Can't Break One Hundred,
     the Problem Is in Your Head, Not Your Aim   154

Imagination                                                     156
Putting                                                         157
The Yips                                                        160
My Trademark Hat                                                161
Presidential Power                                              162
*Lee Trevino on Sam*                                            164
On Practice                                                     167
*Fran Pirozzolo on the Lesson Tee with Sam*                     170
Greensboro: A Favorite Stop                                     171
A Winning "Tree" Wood                                           172
Golf Writers                                                    174
Baseball and Me                                                 176
Holy Cow, I Need to Extend My Arms!                             179
Taking What the Lord Gives Us                                   181
Ryder Cup Captaincy: Team Golf                                  182
School's In                                                     185
Hagen Defeats Hogan                                             187
Star Search: Playing with Celebrities                           189
The Day the Senior PGA Tour Was Born                            193
Golf Course Design                                              195
Pro-Ams                                                         197
Why We Can't Play the Way We Hit It
      on the Practice Tee                                       201
Beyond Golf                                                     202
My Beef with the PGA                                            203
*Dan Quayle on Sam*                                             208
My Eightieth Birthday                                           210
*Fran Pirozzolo on Feel*                                        211
When Something's Not Right About Your Swing                     214
Quayle Hunting                                                  215
The Big Three                                                   216
Arnold Palmer                                                   217

Gary Player                                                      219
Jack Nicklaus                                                    221
Hogan, Nelson, and Me Against Jack Nicklaus
     and the Modern Players                           224
Tiger Cub                                                        226
Tiger Woods                                                      227
Tiger, the Symbol                                                230
Hogan's Secret                                                   231
My Secret                                                        233
Information Overload                                             235
*Mark Steinbauer on Sam*                                         236
Aiming Right                                                     237
Today's Players and Today's Tour                                 238
The Finish of a Good Swing                                       240
Three Contemporary Swings                                        242
Uncle Sam                                                        243
The New Guru                                                     244
Cost-of-Living Increase                                          247
Match-Play Memories                                              248
Augusta Perennial                                                250
My Businesses Today                                              251
Rocks of Ages                                                    253
My Play Today                                                    256


APPENDIX
Sam Snead's Notable Achievements                                 259
Sam Snead's Famous Firsts                                        260
Sam Snead's Tournament Victories                                 261

# ACKNOWLEDGMENTS

Sam and I would like to express our gratitude to the many people who have contributed to the writing of this book. Ann and Jackie Snead have accommodated us and supported our efforts through making available an incredible museum of Sam's old scrapbooks, film, records, and memorabilia. They patiently sat for interviews and provided valuable insights into Sam's career that could not be gotten without their support.

Our special friend, Jack Vardaman, read and critiqued drafts of the manuscript and contributed numerous facts and perspectives that were vital to the initiation, as well as the completion, of the book. Jack's advice and judgment have been invaluable to both of us, in this project and on many others too numerous to mention here.

We are indebted to the players and teachers who provided their commentary on Sam. It should be noted that almost everyone has a ready opinion of the career, swing, and personality of Sam Snead.

We appreciate the willingness of these friends and colleagues to share their thoughts. The comments and insights of Jim McLean, Tom Watson, Judy Rankin, Dick Harmon, Byron Nelson, Lee Trevino, Dan Quayle, and Mark Steinbauer are greatly appreciated.

We thank the Golf Channel and producer Warren Rogan for his support and assistance in providing transcripts, video, and photos that we used in preparing both this book and its sister project, the video entitled *Sam Snead: A Swing for a Lifetime.*

We thank Doug Grad, our editor at Ballantine Books, for his support and patience. His editorial hand has improved the text and made the book better.

We thank Andy Brumer for his lightninglike speed in coming to the rescue when we got down to crunch time.

Finally, we thank Scott Waxman at the Literary Group for his support and encouragement.

*Fran Pirozzolo*

# INTRODUCTION AND SWING DIAGNOSIS

Sam Snead was to golf what Babe Ruth was to baseball—a player so great and so natural that people were awestruck by his immense talent. Sam did things in golf that no one had ever dreamed possible. Like Michael Jordan in basketball, Snead could not only make the seemingly impossible possible, but make it look easy.

Many of the younger generation never saw Sam play or hit a shot, yet Sam played great golf for seven decades. Those of us lucky enough to have seen Snead will never forget it. This book will be a great gift for golfers of all ages, not only for those who did not see him but especially for those who did, to remind them again of his many accomplishments.

Sam simply could do absolutely anything with a golf ball. What made Snead unique was the style and grace in the way he did it. He had *the* golf swing. When you think of the perfect swing, you think of Snead.

When the Golf Channel interviewed Jack Nicklaus, Arnold Palmer, Gary Player, Tom Watson, Lee Trevino, and many other great players for the video *Sam Snead: A Swing for a Lifetime,* they all said Sam had the finest swing in history. Trevino said that his recommendation to juniors learning golf would be to watch a videotape of Snead and try to copy what they saw. He said that would be the best golf lesson they could ever take.

All knowledgeable golfers understand the importance of Sam Snead and his incredible contribution to the game. His list of golf feats is simply beyond comprehension, and many are unlikely to be broken.

It is one thing to have a gift from heaven and entirely another to develop that gift. Snead took his athletic skills and worked a lifetime to become an artist extraordinaire. Sam loved playing golf perhaps more than anybody. At age eighty-five, he still loves to play. In his prime, he rarely missed a day and would tee it up with anybody anytime. Of course, he would expect a little action on the outcome, but he would truly play golf with anyone even when he was the number one player in the world.

As you read about Sam Snead and learn more about this remarkable man, I'm not sure which accomplishments will impress you the most. For me, the fact that he made an ace with every club in his bag (except the putter) and shot sixty—twelve under par—at the Lower Cascades Course at age seventy-one are two of the highlights. Yet there are so many others that could be justifiably more impressive.

You don't hit great golf shots for seventy years without a truly great golf swing. What follows is my analysis of the classic Sam Snead swing from 1950, when Sam was at the top of his game. The innovative "flip-book swing sequence" allows you to see Sam's grace, smoothness, and wonderful tempo—and you can even study the individual pictures to check Sam's swing at any point in the sequence. It's taken from newsreel footage shot at the first tee of the Old White Course at the Greenbrier.

Sam set up on what he called his reverse K address position. His right knee was kicked in, forming part of the reverse K. His left arm and the shaft formed a straight line. With his longer shots, Sam aimed his body a bit right and not parallel to the target line. Snead took the club away in a classic one-piece action. This "everything-away-together" action was a centerpiece of Snead's mechanics.

At the halfway-back position, Sam transferred his weight onto the right leg and swiveled his torso in a powerful coil.

At the three-quarter position in the backswing, Sam took the club slightly inside but pointed right on plane. This is a very natural way to swing the club.

Does it get any better than this? In a word: No.

At the top of the backswing, Sam was coiled beautifully on top of his right leg. In a driver swing, he described his left foot as "only a prop," with most of his weight shifted onto the right side. His left heel was off the ground, and his left knee was pointed well behind the ball. His hands were held high.

As Sam began his downswing, he personified the classic "sit-down" position. Snead's left knee rotated and shuttled toward the target. Because Snead aimed right and then made a huge shoulder turn, his right knee and right side fired more out toward the target line, giving the appearance that the right knee was stationary or even bowing backward. Not true! In fact, Sam said he often felt he pushed off the inside of his right foot for added power.

At impact, his left hip turned clear, pointing left of the target line. His right heel came off the ground. A key swing thought for Snead was to return the club shaft to its original address angle.

After impact, his arms straightened out with the club shaft perfectly between them and pointing to his body center. Snead's right foot slid slightly toward the target.

At the midpoint of the follow-through, Snead's head swiveled toward the target as he stayed on his posture established at address. His spine angle never changed.

At the finish, the club shaft was now behind

Snead and bisected the back of his head. This is the classic finish position, with weight now fully on the left side and eyes looking at the target on a slight tilt. Beautiful.

I have also made comments on some of the individual frames of the flip book sequence. They appear as captions to the left of the pictures.

You have acquired a wonderful book that will provide tremendous insights into a true golf legend. I hope you will enjoy it and refer back to it often.

*Jim McLean*
*Miami, Florida*

# GREETINGS FROM SAM

I was born May 27, 1912. That must have been a good year, because three months earlier, Byron Nelson had been born. Then, three months after me, Ben Hogan was born. Our paths would cross many times along the winding road that came to be known as the PGA Tour.

I have had my share of hardships and misfortune, but overall the past eighty-five years have been very good to me.

I love the game of golf, and I've seen as much as any man in the history of this grand game. Even today, I play a lot of golf—I practice every day, and I get a chance to play about three or four times a week. I don't hit the ball as well as I want—I hurt my left shoulder in a car accident in the late 1980s, and it seems to get weaker every day. I can still shoot even par when my putting cooperates. And I still win almost every bet I make.

In this book I'll tell you what I have come to understand about this game I love, what I've come to understand about myself and the incredible things I've seen in my eighty-five years.

I am often asked how the boys I played with compare to today's generation of players such as Greg Norman, Nick Faldo, and Tiger Woods. I think it's impossible to compare players from one generation to another. The equipment, the courses, the travel, the competition, the challenges of life on the Tour—they're all different.

Life was different in our era. I don't ask that anyone feel sorry for us—just maybe that you try to understand what it might have been like to have played when we did. Just to have lived through what we lived through was remarkable!

# MY FIRST DAY IN GOLF

I guess it was when I was about seven years old in 1919 that some of my friends from Ashwood, Virginia, came by our house and told me they were going to The Homestead to caddie. One of them said they made a lot of money, and it sounded like a good idea. We walked the two and a half miles to The Homestead, and, sure enough, I got to caddie for a lady. I don't remember much about the round, but I do remember after we fin ished she took me up to the hotel and filled my little hat up with pennies and nickels. I scratched around trying to find a dime, but it was all pennies and nickels.

When I got home I found that my mother had begun to worry about me. She had looked all over for me. She thought maybe I had fallen in a stream checking my traplines. She looked all around Ashwood. When I finally came home, she gave me the worst tanning I ever got. I remember pleading, "But, Mom, I brought you all this money." It didn't do much good.

No matter, I was hooked.

# LEARNING TO SWING A CLUB

When you watch a little girl or a little boy take swings at a golf ball you realize that they learn by watching others. They mimic what they see. When people ask how I learned to swing a club, I sense a certain disappointment when I try to explain my natural approach.

The first person I actually played with was my brother, Homer, who was twelve years older than me. We laid out a four-hole course, sank some tomato cans for cups, and hit around rocks with crooked sticks for hours. Homer had a long flowing swing, and he could generate power! I would watch him swing, and I guess you could say I copied his swing. Even at the time, people said we swung the club similarly.

My learning didn't stop there, however. I caddied for Helen Hicks, one of the best women players of the 1920s and '30s. I admired parts of her swing, and I would go off after caddying for her and try to apply a certain part of her swing to mine to see if it would work.

As a young player, I would watch other swings very carefully and try parts of swings I liked to see if they fit with mine. Usually, I ended up discarding the new piece, but it was fun to see what I could invent in my "laboratory." Who knows how it all fit together in the end?

## ADVICE TO PARENTS

One of the troubling things I see in junior golf is that parents get too involved with their kids' golf. They seem to want to be coach, trainer, analyst, and parent. There is too much feedback in golf today, and kids don't have a chance to learn for themselves, to figure out things on their own.

In the early days of the Tour, many wives would travel along with their husbands. They had an expression, "Don't ask him what he shot if he has cockleburs on his pants and sand in his cuffs."

Maybe modern parents could take a lesson from the wisdom of experience gained from the wars on the early Tour. Give a player a chance to relax, forget about the day's bad shots, and just try to enjoy his or her company. Don't try to be a coach.

I've found that kids often do better when they are off playing golf by themselves. You know the way it is: Some kids get together and play, and one says "I'm Jack Nicklaus," or "I'm Tiger Woods," or "This putt is to win the Masters." A camaraderie forms among those kids when they're out there playing together. You can take a kid to a golf course for lessons and it might feel to that kid like he or she is being forced into it. Of course, it is important to let a pro instill the proper fundamentals in a youngster early. But put the emphasis on playing and having fun, not having to perfect what the pro is teaching.

When a child shows interest, and if there is some ability there, then that kid—on his or her own—will want to get at somebody he or she can play against. That's the whole thing, I think: Get children into the right level of competition as early as they can handle it. When talented youngsters don't have a chance to play with other kids of similar ability, then the danger is that they will lose interest in the game because they won't be able to find out how good they really are.

# STICK WITH THE BASICS

Throughout my career I stuck with a system that worked for me. I had my ups and downs, but I am proud of the fact that my approach to the game and my swing worked well for me over the six decades I played competitive golf. I once heard someone say that my swing was one that Charles Darwin would have appreciated—that it withstood the tests of time and competition. Survival of the fittest, right?

Just as new equipment is touted and is used by players eager to jump on the latest bandwagon, many new swing ideas are peddled by the golf magazines. As circumstances change and new ideas and equipment replace the old, what is left are the true basic principles. Usually, players who stick to their systems have the conviction to make those basic principles work for them. The fellows who give up on the basic principles and follow the latest trends, like sheep being herded around, usually get slaughtered.

My basic principles were simple and easy to find when the pressure was on. They helped me reduce tension and get control of myself under pressure.

---

*Fran Pirozzolo on Simplicity*

---

To many players and teachers, Sam Snead was the best example of a natural approach to the golf swing and to playing the game. This proposition is as obvious to some as it is unthinkable to others.

My studies of great athletes, scholars, and leaders have shown that most possess a seemingly contradictory quality of being childlike. As adults, they are uninhibited enough to ask themselves very simple questions, such as *What causes objects to behave the way they do?* Sam embodied this childlike simplicity in innumerable ways, and in this regard he was identical to geniuses in other areas, such as Albert Einstein in physics and Jean Piaget in psychology. In contrast to technicians, who master minor details and find it difficult to simplify, the true geniuses, such as Sam, discover very simple rules (of ball flight, for example) and do not feel particularly burdened by pressures to conform to the fads of the day. In one sense, these extraordinary people dare to be simple. Einstein solved some very simple yet intimidating questions about space and time. He also stated that we know all we ever need to know about physics by the time we are three.

Mac O'Grady, the brilliant player, teacher, and coaching theoretician, told the audience in a PGA Teaching and Coaching Summit that there were nine possible ball-flight directions and trajectories, but only Sam Snead could hit all of the possible shots.

Even today, Sam possesses an incredible child-like quality. Sam spent many thousands of hours in his laboratory (the practice tee) learning how he could make a golf ball behave in a certain way. Once he had discovered these laws of physics, he adapted his behavior (his swing) to the demands that the environment placed on him. Golfers associate this laboratory/scientific approach more with Ben Hogan than Sam Snead, but my guess is that in the future our society will recognize that true genius is more childlike, simple, and uninhibited than we think.

---

# MUSIC AND SWING TEMPO

Everyone who knows me knows I love music. I used my music to help me maintain my swing's rhythm. For me, waltz time, or 3/4 time, was perfect for the correct golf swing tempo. I used to whistle a lot on the course and I feel it kept my timing and rhythm in sync. I had learned that Bobby Jones used musical rhythms to help him keep his swing smooth.

I think the action of the lower body is very important. Footwork is also important, but neither are things to be consciously thinking of while swinging. You should try to hit the ball with a blank mind if possible.

Once, my old pal Toney Penna was having problems driving the golf ball, and he said, "Sam, I can't break seventy-five. I'm hitting it all over the lot with my driver. Do you mind telling me what you see?"

I watched Toney, who had one of my favorite swings, and he was out of rhythm and off balance. I told him that his swing should be like a waltz or slow fox-trot, smooth, easy, flowing. You react to the music.

Toney went out and shot sixty-six the next day and resumed his usual excellence in striking the ball.

Yes, music was and still is a hobby for me. I played several instruments and own a rare Gibson banjo, said to be worth $60,000 today. I always enjoyed dancing and figured that it helped me to learn and to value rhythm and grace.

---

*Tom Watson on Sam's Rhythm*

---

Sam Snead has one of the great swings in golf, and there are many people who believe it was the greatest swing ever. I think if you looked at Sam's swing, his grace and his power, you would have to give him the nod. He had the best swing there ever was.

Of course, I'm prejudiced because my father was a great admirer of Sam's and he would tell me to watch his swing. I grew up knowing a lot about Sam's swing. I would always go out to the practice tee and watch Sam hit balls, especially when I first got out on tour. Invariably, it would help me to watch him swing. It helped my rhythm and my ability to hit the ball by watching him. I've always had a very quick swing, and by watching him practice I think it smoothed out my swing—at least in my own mind.

---

# THE FIRST MATCH

My brother Homer and I would knock stones around our pitch-and-putt course in our yard, but my first serious matches came against my uncle Bud Dudley. We would use Dad's clubs and hack around in the backyard for hours. Sometimes we would use the club that Dad had rigged up for us: an old buggy whip with a wooden head on it. It was good practice for developing hand-eye coordination and for timing.

Uncle Bud was a nice man, and he paid a lot of attention to me. As my mother, Laura, would tell it, I would never sit still, I always had to be moving, doing something. I didn't need supervision, as I was quite an independent fellow. Maybe what I needed was a harness!

I remember one of the first matches we played. I had holed out (in one of Mom's quart-sized tomato cans we had sunk for a hole), and Uncle Bud was swinging away. I said, "How many'd you have, Unc?"

He'd say, "Five."

I'd say, "I think you had nine."

He'd say, "Those were practice swings."

And I'd say, "No. When you grunt it's a stroke, not a practice swing!"

## HAROLD BELL

I owe a lot to Harold Bell, who was one of my coaches at Valley High School. I had visited Virginia Polytechnic Institute, and I was thinking about going to college. I was offered scholarships for football, basketball, baseball, and track. I went to Harold Bell for advice about what to do after high school. He told me he'd given it a lot of thought and said that if I went into golf I'd be way ahead of the game. I wasn't very good at school and I'd be making a living, at least a meager one anyway, if I got into golf right after high school. Making a living was important to us, and I knew I'd be four years behind if I went to college.

Harold Bell taught me some of the best lessons I ever learned. He made me promise I'd never touch liquor, that I'd never lose myself in a bottle of alcohol. I was also discouraged from developing bad habits like smoking, which I never have done. I always took care of my body, and I believe that helped me in the long run. During Prohibition the hills were loaded with moonshiners, and not only did I hate the stuff, but you could get yourself shot at if you ever stumbled upon one of those moon-shiners' stills while you were setting your traps or fishing.

He also taught me the importance of self-control on the course. He gave me the concept of "cool-mad," which I discuss later, which implies that the best approach to your game is to have an intensity about it but not to go over the red line into anger.

# The Importance of
# Physical Conditioning

When I started out on the Tour, the road was a lot bumpier than it is today. Not a single one of us owned our own private jet or helicopter. They hadn't been invented yet! We traveled by car, split gas money, and just as often as not slept in the car while our travel partners drove to the next stop.

It was typical for me to leave my family in January and set out for the West Coast, not to return to them until after the Masters, and then it was time for that big deadline—April 15, tax-filing time! Uncle Sam was always trying to collect what was supposedly buried in the tomato cans in my backyard.

So many of the players of my day were big, strong athletes who had played other sports. You had to be physically strong to endure the punishment of the travel. Tournaments usually ended with thirty-six holes on Sunday, so the players in the best condition had a huge advantage.

I always kept my body in good shape. Every day I had a routine that included stretching, push-ups, and one hundred sit-ups in the morning to keep me toned and limber. I would do some additional push-ups and another hundred sit-ups in the evening. I also did forearm and biceps curls. We didn't have the advantages of the modern players who have a fitness trainer, but we kept strong and fit or we didn't survive the wear and tear.

# LESSONS OF THE HICKORY STICK

There is no doubt in my mind that growing up and playing in the hickory-shaft era was a big advantage for me in developing my swing and my reliance on tempo and timing. In the wooden-shaft days we used hickory, swamp maple, and, in our backyard golf course, anything we could use to attach to a steel head. All wood-shafted clubs had such torque and torsion that you had to wait to feel the club head come into impact. So slow tempo—and an ability to sense where the shaft and head were—were fundamental in my day. A small error in timing sent the ball off so far into the woods you wouldn't even try to find it—except for the fact that real golf balls were so expensive you couldn't afford to lose one.

I was a club maker of hickory-shafted clubs before I turned pro. I could tune a set of hickory-shafted irons with a small pocketknife so that the flex was similar in each club. This was very difficult to do. And in those days, no way would you lean your clubs against the wall when you stored them. You had to lay them down flat or they would warp out of shape!

## The Changeover

One of the hardest things we all had to adjust to in the 1930s was the changeover. We went from the hickory shaft to the steel shaft. The golf swings of the hickory-shafted era were more art than science—

usually involving lots of angles. It took Byron Nelson about five full years to invent a swing that was styled around the stiffer, more consistent steel shaft. Byron reasoned that he wanted the club to move in a straighter line back and through. He was really the first to try to keep the club head on line for a long time. Once he mastered the use of the steel shaft, he thought he was ready for the Tour, and this was in 1933.

# GOALS

Unlike some players, I never really set any goals for myself such as where I wanted to finish on the money list or how many tournaments I wanted to win. Basically, I wanted to win every tournament, and I set my sights on that each week.

I felt that if I was in shape, if my game was in shape, I would be fine. When Jack Nicklaus came along I remember how he planned his schedule around his preparation for the majors. I never did that. I never thought much about the Open or the Masters until I got there. I did hope to be playing well before I got there. That would eliminate the number of things I needed to worry about in my game.

I don't think that you can point to a tournament and say, "That's the one I'm going to win." I don't think you can make it happen, although that's no reason not to give it your best shot.

I always felt that I could handle the pressure of the big ones. I liked playing against the best players in the world. For instance, playing with Hogan, I always felt I could come up a notch or two against him. Against players like Hogan and Nelson you knew you had to play well to win. You knew going in it was going to be tight, so your goal was right there in front of you: Play the best you know how!

# BEING SURROUNDED BY OTHERS WHO BELIEVE IN YOU

I think it's so important that you associate with the right kind of people. I often hear fellows say that they don't enjoy their golf game because they're playing with this guy or that guy. For amateurs especially, golf is supposed to be fun. Why would you play with someone you know is going to make you miserable?

It is truly a blessing when the family you grow up in believes in you. Coming from a big family (I was the youngest of six children), where my dad worked hard and my mom worked hard, I learned to take care of my own affairs at a young age. My father was a big, strong man who worked as an all-purpose handyman, electrician, and what-not for a hotel in town. He was also a Bible teacher—quiet, strong as an ox, and with incredible powers of concentration.

My mother was much closer to us kids than Dad,

of course, because she was always taking care of us. She was physically very strong, and smart, although, like most women of that time, she never finished grade school. She was forty-seven when I was born, and so a lot of the responsibility of raising me, the baby of the family, went to my sister, Jenny.

Jenny's real name was Janet, but she went by Jenny, a name she liked better. My brother Welford didn't like his name, so we called him Pete. Jesse (whose real name is Jesse James Snead) came to be known as Jess, and I wanted to be called Jack, but my family insisted on staying with Sam. My middle name is Jackson, after a grandfather who knew Confederate general Stonewall Jackson.

Jenny made me believe I was someone special—that I might have special talents that no one else had. She always told me I could do anything I put my mind to and, by golly, I tried to prove she was right!

It's funny how the people around you can influence you to do great things. I remember, in 1965, right before I won Greensboro for the eighth time when I was fifty-three years old, Ed Sullivan said, "Wouldn't it be great if Sam could win this championship for the eighth time?" When he said that I felt as if my whole being was raised up. I said to myself that night, "I'm going to give it an extra shot and really try to make it happen." And I won by four shots!

Now, I never heard my mother or father say,

"We love you," but I had the feeling they did, that they'd die for us. I could see by the way they acted that they loved us. I would press my mom by telling her that I was nobody's favorite. "Your favorite is Jess, and Pop's is Homer," I would say.

She would reply, "No, we love one as much as the other."

## STRINGS AND STONES

Growing up using anything we could to hit a golf ball, or a stone for that matter, we probably developed more feel for the game, more feel for our clubs, than kids today. We would put a stone on the end of a string and swing it, sensing where the stone was before we released. I grew up in the hickory-shaft era, when the clubs were very whippy and heads were relatively heavy. I always believed this was a huge advantage for me because it helped me to develop good timing, tempo, and feel of the club head.

Bobby Jones used exclusively hickory-shafted

clubs in his day, and he had wonderful rhythm, timing, and feel of the club head. When he retired, people said his clubs were tested scientifically for all the technical-sounding specifications we hear about today, such as swing weight and frequency. They were all identical, except for his mashie-niblick, which Bob said he could never hit worth a darn anyway.

I know that I developed such an awareness of the way clubs felt that you could blindfold me and put a barrel full of drivers in front of me and I could find my original Dunlop Gold Cup driver every time. I remember Ben Hogan saying much the same thing. Once he got his hands on clubs that felt right, he could make them sing.

Here's an interesting little footnote. Wilson, at that time, made woods for Dunlop with the Dunlop name on them. Years later, Wilson put a Wilson sole plate on my Gold Cup Driver since I was a member of the Wilson staff and have represented them since 1937.

# DEPRIVATION AS A COMPETITIVE ADVANTAGE

Because of the way we grew up in my era, I believe we had more desire, more hunger, a greater *need* to play well. So many of the players of my day were deprived as youngsters. We needed to play. We needed to win. We had lived through several world-wide deprivations—World War I, the Great Depression, World War II. Kids today can't appreciate what it was like to go to bed at night in fear that the world as we knew it might be drastically changed when we woke up in the morning.

Growing up in the mountains of Virginia was no day at the beach, either. I was basically on my own, and I supported myself by the time I was nine or ten.

Do kids who are raised without ever knowing how to fight for themselves, or how to confront their fears, have the same desire to win?

# EXTRAORDINARY EXPERIENCES

There is no question in my mind but that I was blessed with some special talents and skills. I think everyone is blessed with some special something that the Lord gives them. The important thing is what you do with that gift—how you train it, how you use it—if you decide to use it at all.

Some people assume that because I tried to keep my approach simple and natural I just fell off that turnip truck on the winter tour of 1937 and started winning tournaments. I don't think anything could be further from the truth.

I worked at it. I practiced as much as anyone, with the possible exception of Hogan. I worked at my fitness and conditioning. I was careful about my diet and didn't drink or smoke cigarettes.

To understand why I have succeeded (and failed), you have to understand the training of a mountain boy. The experiences I had shaped and molded my skills. The stories that were written about me were for the most part true. I was a hillbilly, and I never considered going to Harvard or Princeton to study physics in the hope that I could beat out Albert Einstein in the race to understand relativity.

My young life, with its emphasis on survival in nature—on hunting and fishing—demanded that I develop skills that would put me in tune with what was going on out there. When you trap wild animals, when you learn to catch fish using your bare hands, you learn to be quiet, to feel with all of your senses. I tried to develop these senses and the imagery that went with them into a way of mastering the environment. I can't explain why I am able to stick my hand in a pond and have a bass take hold of it or why I am able to pick that bass out of the water and rub its belly. I don't know—but I don't question it, either. I think a great gift I have been given is a certain childlike appreciation of the natural world.

I remember something Jack Fleck said about his 1955 victory over Hogan in the U.S. Open at the Olympic Club. It was one of the all-time greatest upsets in the history of the game: You know, unknown driving-range pro beats world's best golfer! How did he do it? He said as he looked at the hole, the hole became as big as a washtub. He convinced himself he couldn't miss, and he sustained this conviction by not questioning it.

There were many times when my senses seemed to blend with each other, giving them richer expression. I felt my swing to be oily. I could sense what other players were thinking at times. I could hear the rhythm of my swing. And when I was overgolfed, I tasted a salty taste in my mouth.

# THE FIRST LESSON

Like anyone who wanted to be a golf pro, I started out making clubs. I was apprentice to Freddy Gleim, who was the head pro at The Homestead. This was 1934, when I was twenty-two years old. I was earning the princely sum of twenty dollars a month. I would clean clubs and repair them, sticking steel heads on hickory shafts. I got to be fairly good at making and repairing clubs. The young fellows in the shop got to go out and play early in the morning, but we had to be in the shop by 8 A.M.

The Homestead, of course, catered to some well-to-do people, many of whom would want to take a tennis or golf lesson. One day, a rich, fat lady came into the shop and asked for a lesson. The pros were all out teaching or playing, so I agreed to give her a lesson.

I took her out to the practice area and showed her how to put her hands on the club. She really did well, worked hard. She told me it was the best lesson she'd ever had. She marched smartly down to The Homestead and spoke to Mr. Ingals, who owned the hotel. She told him that she had just gotten the best lesson ever, from a young fellow who should be on the professional staff!

I then was hired as the apprentice professional at the Cascades Course. I set the course record that summer by shooting a sixty-one. This is still the record today.

# ADVICE TO TEACHERS OF THE GAME

My life in golf has been very rewarding, but winning tournaments, attaining a certain status, and playing with presidents were not all that have given me great pleasure. The teaching I've done, and the ability to help another golfer enjoy this game more, have been gifts I've received, as well as given. To this day, while I don't give formal lessons anymore, I get a great kick out of helping a player understand himself and his method better. Being a professional is very important to me, and I think it brings certain responsibilities.

There have always been great teachers in the game of golf, and most people have never heard of them. Stewart Maiden was a great teacher to Bob Jones, and the only reason you've ever heard of him is because of the credit Bob gave to Maiden for helping him shape his game. Stewart taught Bob the fundamentals that were important—very simple things that today wouldn't make it into the golf magazines because they seem ridiculously simple and natural.

Stewart apparently understood two subjects: golf and Bob Jones.

I think golf professionals today have more technical knowledge than at any other time in the history of this royal and ancient game. I don't feel that some teachers "put it all together" so they can really help players improve mentally and physically. Then, of course, it is not always easy to help a player. Novice players are easy to teach. They usually pay close attention to what their pro tells them and faithfully carry out the study and the practice of the game.

Unfortunately, most other players are not easy to help because they have filled their heads up with opinions, ideas, and explanations for just about everything related to golf. As students, they fail the course. They've usually taken plenty of lessons from other pros and don't give a new instructor a fair chance to help them.

I sympathize with instructors who try to come up with new information or new technology to teach this old game. But I don't agree with teachers who don't take their responsibilities seriously enough to teach the Basic Fundamentals to each player.

The golf instructor should be, above and beyond all other things, a "Father Confessor" of golf. The golfer should be able to take all of his golf troubles to his teacher and have the teacher listen with respect and set about to resolve the difficulties the player is having. The teacher should want the player to enjoy the game and play it to the best of his or her ability.

I enjoy helping the pros on tour today and have been getting a lot of calls lately to look at their swings. They realize that I have been where they are in a competitive situation both mentally and physically. Some of the teachers today haven't had this experience and don't understand what it is like to be under the gun. I try to give today's players something to use for their swing that works under pressure. The good Lord knows I have been there and have had some experience at it.

I gave Tom Watson a lesson in 1996, one week

before he won at Muirfield, Ohio, his first win on the Tour in nine years. And I gave Tom Kite a lesson one week before the 1997 Masters. Tom came in second behind Tiger Woods.

# COVERING THE STRIKE ZONE

Every player who plays this game is different. Humans come in all shapes and sizes. The Lord sees to it that that happens.

For my era, I was a little taller than the average guy at five-foot-eleven, but I had very long arms. I wear a thirty-five-inch sleeve. Other guys were taller or shorter with different-length arms. Ben Hogan was short, but with very long arms for his size. Ben used clubs that were shorter than the standard length.

Every player should be fitted for clubs and not assume that he or she needs a standard set. I've played golf with hundreds of professional athletes, and most times they've shown up with standard-length clubs. Most of the tall guys were hunched over the ball, in very bad posture, and couldn't consistently make a good solid hit.

Would a baseball player use a bat that was so short it didn't reach the outside half of the plate? No. Then why would a golfer use a club that, once he got in a good athletic setup, didn't reach the ball, golf's strike zone?

# THE CASCADES OPEN—1935

I decided I was playing well enough to enter a tournament at The Cascades. Some fellows thought I was foolish, but I thought I could win.

We had quite a field. Some of the major players of the day were there: Johnny Farrell, Craig Wood, and Billy Burke, for instance. I was leading by three going into the final round. The first hole at the Upper Cascades is basically the same as it is today, except in 1935 the green was in front.

Back then I had a very strong grip and used a

two and a half wood—I couldn't hit a driver because it hooked too much. I drove the first green, which was about 320 yards. I two-putted for a birdie and a four-stroke lead.

Well, the head pro and some others had said to themselves, "Snead can't win. An unknown pro can't be allowed to win our tournament. What would people think?"

Walking across the road as you have to in order to get to the second tee, Freddy Gleim, the head pro, gave me the needle. He said, "Sam, your left arm is coming away from your chest. You're going to hook the ball!"

Well, I thought, Why would he say that to me now? And I promptly hooked my drive into the trees on the left of the fairway. I have a picture of myself scowling, walking off that tee box. I ended up third.

Gleim didn't want me to win, because I was unknown at that time and The Homestead wanted good press with a known champion for the resort's profit.

# THE GRIP

One of the first fundamentals is probably the most troublesome for the average player, and that is the grip. It is important to remember that the only connection the golfer has with the golf club is through his hands—through the grip. The grip has to deliver the club face to the ball in a fairly square position time after time, and it ought to do it with some *speed.*

If you are right-handed, the left-hand grip should run from the last joint of the forefinger, across the hand, and under the base or heel pad of the hand. Too many amateurs let the club run diagonally too high into the heel pad of the left hand. With a left-hand grip too high up in the heel pad, you can't cock the wrists very well, and that could cause you to lose control of the club or "throw" it from the top of the backswing. You certainly can't create speed or snap with a poor left-hand grip.

The left thumb should be on the right side of the

grip, *not* on top of the grip as some pros teach. Again, you can't hinge and hold the club well with your thumb on the top. You should be able to hold the club with the last two fingers of your left hand and balance the shaft under the heel pad.

Grip pressure is very important. You can't strangle the club with a hog killer's grip. You've got to hold it as if it were a little bird—gently but firmly. You don't want it to fly away, but you don't want to suffocate the poor thing, either. Proper grip pressure that stays constant throughout the swing enables you to swing more consistently.

The right-hand grip is a finger grip. The right index finger should form a little trigger-finger look on the grip. The Vs of both hands should point toward the right shoulder. The right pinkie, in the Vardon or overlapping grip, fits in the slot between your left index and middle fingers, enabling your hands to work together and not fight each other. I definitely think the Vardon grip is the best, but I have no problem with players who have smaller hands or stubby fingers using a baseball grip or an interlocking grip.

The main thing is delivering the club head to the ball in a free and easy manner that allows the wrists to hinge correctly.

# NEVER GIVE UP—NEVER GIVE IN

I learned some of the most important lessons I would ever learn as soon as I started out to play in the "big leagues." I had played in only three amateur tournaments in my high school career, all nine-holers, and never won anything. I think I finished third once. But in 1936 I set out on my journey to get a look at the big boys.

My first event was in Hershey, Pennsylvania. I took my first train ride up there, getting lost in Pennsylvania Station in New York a few times trying to find the right train to Hershey.

Eventually, I showed up all set for a practice round with my old worn golf bag and a set of eight (yes, eight) clubs in my bag. On the first tee I joined a group, including a nice man who I later discovered was George Fazio. He told me that the first hole was a 345-yard par four and that I should just play it straight. With six eyes staring at me, I made a huge

34

swing, sending the ball into the chocolate factory off to the right of the number one fairway. Unplayable. I hit another with the same result. I topped the third just in front of the tee. I can remember thinking that I had had about all the professional golf I could stand right there in my first event.

Fazio was very sensitive to my nervousness. I wanted to quit and go home, but George quietly said, "Hit another, son." I slowed myself down enough to make a more normal swing and launched my tee shot.

One of the other pros said, "My God, he's on the green!" And when we reached the green, 345 yards away, sure enough, there was my ball twenty feet from the pin.

This was a lesson I would have to keep in mind. Surely there would be other adversities I'd have to face in the future that would make me want to give in. Persistence, determination, and eliminating any tendency to want to quit when things get rough are important qualities for golfers.

I always tried to remind myself of the great number of times I would follow a sequence of poor shots with a good one—or even a great one. As long as this was a possibility, I reasoned, then why not *expect* good ones to follow bad ones—especially off the tee, where you can recover with good iron shots, chips, or putts and still have a good hole?

# GIVING UP

I did give up a little later on the Tour, and I regret it. In 1938, on the West Coast swing I seemed to get paired with Jimmy Thomson in each event. Jimmy, of course, shared billing with me as "the longest humans." The promoters of the events wanted to see us paired together to see who was the longest driver of a golf ball. Well, I wasn't about to be outdriven, and neither was he. We both got out of our rhythms time and again, and the scores kept getting higher.

At the Paradise Open I was paired with Thomson again. Finally, I couldn't take it anymore. I shot forty-one on the front, and, at the twelfth hole, I hit a vicious hook under a tree. I said, "That's it. I'm through." I picked up my ball and left town. I did it again in the next event, at Pinehurst, and I came in for some heavy criticism. My thinking was that I didn't want to make a fool of myself by playing poorly, so I quit. I finally realized what so many others had realized before me. It's not right to be a quitter. It's a loser's way of thinking. You should take your medicine and not get caught up in false pride.

I knew this had happened to Bobby Jones in the British Open, to Tommy Armour in the U.S. Open, and to Gene Sarazen in the Masters. It would happen to Arnold Palmer in 1955 in the Cavalcade of Golf and the Mayfair and in the Motor City Open, but he, like me, cured himself forever.

In recent days we've seen John Daly pick up his ball and walk off far too many times. Why this seems to happen to the aggressive, power-type player more than others I'll never know. But as we've all learned, it is a bad idea.

# THE ORIGINAL BIG BERTHA

If you ask a golfer today about the "Big Bertha," chances are he'll tell you about the very popular driver made by Callaway. But I'll bet you don't know who the original Big Bertha of Golf was. And younger folks who haven't studied their history books won't know what the Big Bertha actually was, but we old folks can surely recall it.

During World War I, Imperial Germany spent millions of dollars developing munitions in an effort to conquer Europe. The Krupp factory turned out all sorts of new and horrible killing machines, and one of them was Big Bertha, a huge cannon that used two-thousand-pound shells and could shell Paris from fifty miles away. Big Bertha was loaded on a railway car and took hundreds of soldiers to operate. It got its nickname from the heir to the Krupp armament works, whose name was Bertha. When I arrived on the Tour, articles were written about me saying that I was the Big Bertha of Golf.

Newspapers from Scotland, reporting on the 1937 Ryder Cup matches in Southport, England, printed my picture with the caption calling me "The Big Bertha of Golf" because of my length off the tee. I averaged over three hundred yards with my tee shots during my first Ryder Cup.

To illustrate how long I was in my early years, I'll relate this little story. I was paired with Gene Sarazen at Hershey in 1936. I was hitting it pretty long with my three wood, maybe three hundred yards or so. After we played, Sarazen told the pro at Hershey that he had just finished watching a kid who didn't know the first thing about *playing golf* but that he didn't want to be around when I learned.

I won maybe 80 or 90 percent of the long-drive contests in those days. I won the PGA driving contest in 1937, hitting three balls a total of 1,005 yards in an enclosed fairway area, averaging 335 yards each with the poor-quality balls and shafts of that time compared to what we play with today.

## FOR EXTRA DISTANCE

As hard as it may seem to understand, when I really wanted to hit it a long way—say, in a driving contest or a par five without any out-of-bounds—I would try to swing *slower,* not faster. I heard Jack Nicklaus say this when he came up, too.

I would try to make a bigger turn by going a little slower. When I went slower, I felt I could get the club into a good position and return it square to the line I wanted the ball to travel on.

# MORE THOUGHTS ABOUT THE GRIP

When people say golf is the hardest to play of all the sports, I think you can relate that right back to the grip. Think about it. If your club face is open just a little bit, even if you swing the club perfectly, the ball goes to the right. Now if the face is closed up a little bit and you make a great swing, it's going to the left. As I said, the hands control the club face, and this reverts back to the grip. A good sound grip allows that club face to return squarely to the ball.

The average player has a terrible grip! Most people's grips are too weak in the left hand, with the hand turned too much to the left. Then they combine that with a strong right-hand grip, with the hand turned to the right, and now the left hand can't contain the power or force of the right and they're in trouble!

I think this will help. The butt or muscular heel pad of your left hand has got to be positioned on top of the shaft or grip so that it doesn't move back and forth or in and out during the swing. Don't put that grip of the club on top or across the heel pad, put the heel pad on top of the club's grip and keep your left hand secure and closed through the swing. Especially when you're in the rough, you need a good stable left-hand grip to keep that club from turning over when it gets caught in the grass. When people wear a hole in their glove there in the heel pad, why, that's a sign of a bad grip. That means the club is on top of, not under, that heel pad. I've never worn a glove out at the heel.

There have been different fashions as far as the grip goes over the years. For example, it seems that back in the late 1960s and 1970s, a weak left-hand grip was in. Hogan had rotated his left hand more to the left, so everybody wanted to do it. But Hogan did it to fight a hook, and what it did to the poor amateur was accentuate his slice! Now, most top players favor a stronger grip with the left hand, and I'll tell you why I like it. For the higher handicapper, it lessens that tendency to slice. For the better players, rotating that left hand over to the right a little gives it more room to roll over or move through impact. The more it moves, the more swing speed it helps generate and the farther you are going to hit the ball.

When all is said and done, you can't argue with more distance. People just don't like to hear those words: "You're away."

# BOBBY JONES

The first time I ever played with Bobby Jones was thrilling—in more ways than one. I had always admired Bob, and, of course, I knew a little about his game: He was the best player in history. Many people compared our games, saying we were the best natural players.

The way our first round came about was that I was contacted by Fred Corcoran, who was the tournament director of the PGA at the time. Fred said, "Bob wants to play with you at Augusta." I said I would be happy to go there, then he told me that we would be traveling by airplane. Up until that time I had never been on an airplane, and I was convinced that I didn't want to fly. But it was an opportunity to play with an idol. I agreed to go along with Fred, and we boarded one of those open-cockpit models. We were going from Greensboro to Augusta, which today, in modern jets, you wouldn't worry about a bit. But there were no safety devices then, such as radar. The pilot navigated his way using a Shell Oil road map that sat in his lap! He would spot landmarks by peering out of the airplane and checking them off on the map.

I wish I could have seen Bobby Jones play in his prime. By the time I came into the game he had retired, and he later became disabled with syringomyelia, a degenerative disease of the spinal cord. I played twice with Bobby, the first time in our round at Augusta and once in a Red Cross match. Even then he was a good driver of the golf ball and was great around the greens. Some say he was the best putter ever as well. However, he didn't hit his long irons particularly well that first day.

I never tried to copy anything he did, but I did see some similarities in the way we played. We both had good tempo and rhythm. We took the club back slowly, almost dragging the club head behind our hands (as opposed to an early wrist cock some of the boys use today). It seemed as if Bobby also lined up a little right and swung down slightly outside his backswing plane.

They say he was magical when his Calamity Jane putter got hot! About our only similarity here is that I also used an old Calamity Jane putter that I'd bought from Henry Picard my first year on the Tour in 1937.

After my putting touch started deteriorating, I discovered that I could putt better by standing behind the line of the putt and putting croquet-style, and I received quite a bit of attention. When I went to Augusta for the Masters, Bobby Jones told me that my croquet-style putting looked bad. He said, "Sam, stop that. That doesn't look like golf!"

I told him, "Bob, nobody asks you how you looked, just how you shot!" Although I never found out, I always suspected that Bob started the discussion that resulted in the USGA ruling that a player couldn't stand behind his line and putt croquet-style.

I made a slight adjustment to stand off the line and putt in a manner that become known as side-saddle, something I do to this day.

# BEST DRESSED AND WELL FED

When I used to work at the Greenbrier, they made us wear a shirt and tie. Well, I got so used to it, I wore a shirt and tie, along with a sleeveless sweater, when I played in my first U.S. Open at Oakland Hills. I might not have won the tournament, but I did get named the best-dressed golfer of the tournament.

With all the logos those guys have on their clothes these days, I'm not sure anyone could get away with giving out such an award anymore.

Eventually, I stopped playing in a shirt and tie, but I got to work on my fashion statements, as you might call them, by changing the broad band on my hat fairly often.

I've been told that I was the first one to receive the green jacket when I won the 1949 Masters. I can't honestly say that I remember that to be the case, but I'm mighty proud indeed of a picture hanging on my wall of me and a group of other Masters champions all in our green jackets. But you can't take that jacket off the premises at Augusta National.

One thing I'm certain of is that Ben Hogan started the tradition of the Champions Dinner. On the Tuesday night before the tournament starts, Augusta National holds a dinner in honor of the previous year's winner, with all past Masters champions attending.

Hogan thought that the guy who wins the tournament must pay for dinner for the other champions the next year. What the heck, today a guy gets a few hundred thousand dollars for winning the Masters, you mean he can't afford to pay for dinner?

# GRIP PRESSURE

I always tried to grip the club with a very light grip pressure. I never developed calluses on my hands, because I kept my hands light and soft on the club. You could probably take my club away from me at the top of the backswing, I gripped it so lightly. I think that with light grip pressure, you can get more zip and better release at impact for more distance.

You watch hitters in baseball. When the bat goes back and waggles, their wrists are oily and light. They get more pop when they have that lightness.

Chi Chi Rodriguez was having problems driving the ball a while back. He is a long hitter for his size, but he was losing distance, not driving it as far as usual. He told me that he couldn't hit it very far anymore and asked me for some help.

I took Chi Chi to the other side of the golf course, and all we worked on was light grip pressure. Next day, Chi Chi hit the ball more solidly and birdied six holes on his back nine. Sometimes we don't realize how tension and pressure build up and give us bad habits like gripping the club too firmly.

# COMPANY MAN

Wilson signed me to an endorsement contract in 1937, and to this day, sixty years later, I'm still with them. The president of Wilson then was L. B. Icely. I treated him as if he were my daddy. In fact, he was the guy who signed me up.

I went in there, and he said, "We have the best irons and woods."

And I said, "Uh-huh." I told him, "You want to know the truth? Then go out there and look in the players' bags and see what they're using. I don't want you to send anyone else. I want you to go."

Later, I told him, "Hey, you're not selling enough woods." I had a guy from Wilson come into the pro shop and take back the best set of woods I had ever seen. Well, they used those clubs as a model, and then they started to sell the heck out of the clubs. As for that set of mine they used, well, I never saw them again.

Hogan started his own company, and at one point I was offered the top spot as an equipment manufacturer. But I really wasn't deeply into club design the way Hogan was.

## GAINING AN EDGE

Wilson made and continues to make wonderful clubs that I still use to this day. But when I wanted to do some work on my clubs, I did it myself; I didn't send them back to Wilson. It was important to get the leading edge of the irons, the bottom of the club that faces the ball, just right.

I rolled the edges of my irons. If the edge is too sharp, it will dig into the ground when you hit the ball. In other words, if you hit it a little fat, or too far behind the ball, the club will keep going down through the ground and you'll have a poor shot. In fact, nowadays a lot of the manufacturers build their irons with a little bounce on that leading edge so it can't get down into the ground too much. Well, I think that's the way all clubs should be made.

Lawson Little had a set of irons from Spalding whose leading edges were as round as shafts. They had no edge on them at all, and I'll tell you what, he didn't hit very many fat ones with those clubs. They would slide on into the ball. Some players take divots so deep you can see all the way down to China.

When I finally got my clubs right, I held on to them. I played a set of clubs for twenty years. By the time I was through with them, I didn't have any grooves on the long irons, right up to the five iron. What the heck—you don't need any grooves on the face of your irons to put spin on the ball. The USGA proved that with its testing.

In fact, the face on my pitching wedge became sort of concave from hitting so many shots with it over the years. All of the irons had a round spot right in the middle of the face.

I did have problems with my seven iron, though, and to this day, I can't figure it out. I'd hook that thing, and I'd beat it on the ground. I'd bend it to adjust the lie angle; I did everything to the club you could think of to try to get that hook shot out of it. I mean, I wouldn't hook the six iron or the eight iron, but that seven iron . . . It could have been the shaft, because I never did switch it. A lot of times, I'd hit a hard eight or an easy six. I'd play around it and wouldn't even use the seven.

Bob Hope once said that in my career I went through fifty sets of Wilson clubs and one hat. It was funny, but in reality, Bob got it reversed. I used a set that I liked for as long as I could, but I wore out about a dozen hats a year!

I knew a player who hit one of his irons a good two clubs farther than he should have. I don't recall which club had that extra kick in it, but if it was his eight iron, it would have gone farther than his six iron. Whichever one it was, some tests were done on it, and it was found out that the iron in question was actually made of a different type of metal than his others. If he had all of his irons made with that metal, he never would have had to use anything more than a four iron!

Some club problems are better to have than others, I guess.

---

*Judy Rankin on the One-Piece Takeaway*

---

I learned to play golf as a little girl in the early fifties, the height of the careers of Ben Hogan and Sam Snead. The people who taught me always stressed paying attention to the rigid swing mechanics of Hogan. But Sam Snead's swing was one that everyone admired. It had great beauty and rhythm.

We were taught that the swing should begin in one piece, that everything moves back together. Many teachers believe that this is the correct way to get started.

Sam was the kind of champion who could accomplish the one-piece takeaway. He started everything away together in a rhythmical manner. Sam's swing never seemed too mechanical. It didn't seem like something he learned but something that was natural for him.

Golfers can learn a lot from Sam's swing. Try to attain the same rhythm—one that is natural for you—and you will have a much better chance of being repetitive. That is the real trick of the game: to find something that works and to be able to repeat it.

Sam didn't seem to try the different mechanics that might have been the fad of that particular day. He just stuck with what worked for him.

# THE ATHLETIC START-UP
## TO THE SWING

I think that the start to the swing is very important. Most amateurs tend to jerk the club back, thus destroying any timing they have.

I prefer a one-piece takeaway. I think players do better over a longer period with a slow, one-piece takeaway. Jones, Hagen, Nelson, Hogan—they all did it this way. Very few players of my era "broke their wrists" early in the takeaway. Jerry Barber did it, and he didn't do badly for a while, but very few others did. I felt if you loaded your wrists early you could get into hooking the ball something awful!

Start with a nice little push forward, a waggle or forward press, we call it, then rebound into your backswing. When you watch a baseball pitcher, you see this. In order to start his movement—to get his motor going—he goes forward first, then back, then forward and pop! It's the same way in golf. When you address the ball and just stand there it builds up pressure in the hands, wrists, and arms. This makes it hard to take the club back smoothly and slowly.

If you have a little looseness, that little forward press, then you can start your swing better. I rarely see amateurs do this part well. The average player would improve a lot by trying this athletic start.

# THE RYDER CUP

I think the Ryder Cup is one of the best events in all of golf. I was a member of ten Ryder Cup teams. My very first one was in 1937. We didn't play the matches during the war, so I only got to play in nine.

The Ryder Cup has come a long way since that time, and I am glad to see that all of Europe and not just Great Britain and Ireland make up a team to play the U.S. I think it's more like the Olympics now. It's a real honor to represent your country.

I almost didn't make it on the team in 1937. I was one of the last players named, because some people felt I might not be able to handle the pressure.

Walter Hagen was the captain but, for the first time in Ryder Cup history, didn't play. Some of my teammates were Gene Sarazen, Henry Picard, Byron Nelson, Horton Smith, and Johnny Revolta. The matches were played in Southport, England.

Well, I did handle the pressure in Ryder Cup play, and I've won more matches than any other player. I've had some bad ones, too. The painful memory is of a 1953 match against Harry Weetman. I had never lost a match in Ryder Cup play up to that point, and I had Weetman down by four holes, going to our thirty-first hole. I lost the thirty-first. On the thirty-second I couldn't get up and down. On the thirty-third I took a six. On the thirty-fourth I took another six. On the thirty-fifth I made a five to Weetman's birdie four. On the final hole we tied, giving Weetman a one-up victory.

Probably the most controversial moment in Ryder Cup play involved Jack Nicklaus, Tony Jacklin, and me in 1969. I was the U.S. Team captain for the third time, the other two times being 1951 and 1959. Jack and Tony were playing the decisive final match. If Jack won, we won. If not, we tied the Brits.

In a poignant moment of good sportsmanship, Jack conceded a three-and-a-half-foot putt to Jacklin to result in a tied match on the final hole. I felt it was too much of a concession to make—given the circumstances—and Jack felt it was the right thing to do. We agreed to disagree.

# THE PLANE TRUTH

There is no question that a golfer's plane, that is, the arc of his backswing and downswing, is very important. It *always has been,* although ideas about it have changed from year to year. Hogan, in modern times, made the swing plane a popular teaching idea. But before Hogan there were Seymour Dunn, Alex Morrison, and a whole lot of Scots who had some simple ideas on plane.

I tried to make it as simple as I could. I wanted the shaft to go up and down on the same plane— occupying the same space, I used to say. The Scots used to teach that on the backswing, you put your left thumb in your right ear and in the finish you put your right thumb in your left ear. If you do that, you have a perfect arc.

I didn't necessarily think about the arc in my swing, but I felt that when I wasn't returning to the ball in a good position, it was because my swing back and up wasn't right. I wanted to return the shaft to the position it started up in, and, when my backswing wasn't up enough, I got over the top on the way down and would hit some funny shots. I don't think the exact plane is that important—just have your hands between your shoulder and your ear at the top and the same on the follow-through.

# THE 1938 PGA: I GET A SHORT-GAME LESSON

While the 1942 PGA Championship was probably the most important victory to me, there were other PGA Championships that were very significant for many different reasons. Of course, the PGA Championship is significant in its own right—it's the championship of the PGA of America. It was always a long, tough battle, as you had to play thirty-six holes of a qualifying round and then thirty-six holes in each match, starting with the quarterfinals some years, and in the third round in others. The format was changed to medal play in 1958. It was typically played on great courses such as Oakmont, where I won in 1951; Cherry Hills, where I was a quarter-finalist in 1941; Oakland Hills, where I tied for fourth in 1972; Canterbury, where I finished tied for ninth in 1973; and Tanglewood, where I tied for third in 1974, at the age of sixty-two!

I had a good run of PGA Championships—they were grueling, but they seemed to fit my game. It seemed as if something significant happened to me almost every year. In 1948, Claude Harmon and I played the longest-ever quarterfinal match in the history of the championship. He shot a sixty-four in the morning against me, and I put up a sixty-four in the afternoon to tie him. On the first extra hole, I had a seven-footer for a birdie to win, but Claude placed a dead stymie against me and we tied the hole. On the forty-second hole we both had twenty-footers for birdie, but he made his putt and I missed mine, ending the match. Jim Turnesa beat Claude in the semifinals the next day.

I was favored to win the 1938 PGA at the Shawnee Country Club in Pennsylvania, and I reached the finals against Paul Runyan. I was a ten-to-one favorite to whip him. Paul was a little fellow who had a great short game and loved beating bigger fish. It was sweltering that week in the Delaware Valley—over one hundred degrees. Paul would sit in a tub of cold water to cool his body down so he could handle the heat better. He even did it between rounds, because there was usually a two-hour period between the morning and afternoon rounds.

It was frustrating driving the ball a hundred yards past Runyan on the par fours and fives and then losing to his magical short game. As a matter of fact, I never birdied any one of the par fives, while he birdied five of six. I ended up hitting over the back of the greens and finding myself pitching from heavy rough. I admired what Runyan did, in spite of the fact that I lost a great chance to win my first major.

# THE WEDGE

I think the club I played best from the beginning of my career until the end was the wedge. I know that many of the players I played with thought I was the best wedge player ever.

I had two secrets. The first, which few people know to this day, is that I used a pitching wedge for almost all of my pitch shots from the fairway. I didn't use the sand wedge as most players did inside one hundred yards. I would use the sand wedge only if I had to hit a very high shot.

The sand wedge was made to hit out of the sand. It has bounce on it, on the bottom of the club, so that it skids through the sand. You are taking a chance—especially if you're an amateur—if the ground is hard. You can hit it fat, or worse, blade it about two hundred yards.

Today, because of the new loft standards, manufacturers make pitching wedges with forty-eight degrees, which would have been a nine iron during my prime. My pitching wedge had fifty-two degrees of loft, so it was very adequate to hit high shots.

The second secret was, of course, practice. I hit hundreds of wedge shots every week from all different distances—50, 70, 90, 105 yards. I got to the point where I could feel the distance in my swing. You don't need to be a pro to try this. It's a tremendous way to get a feel for your swing and develop a real scoring shot.

*Dick Harmon on Sam's Wedge Play*

Sam Snead was a wonderful player. I always enjoyed watching his tempo and rhythm. The most vivid memories I have of Sam are of observing his wedge game. He may have been the best

59

ever with a wedge. He had great feel for his wedge game. I remember watching him walk into a bunker with such an air of confidence. He said, "Watch this, I'm going to put the 'airstairs' on this shot." He could make his bunker shots climb up the stairs and drop straight down, something that I thought he and my dad, Claude Harmon, did as well as anyone in the history of the game.

---

# LIGHTHORSE HARRY COOPER

Lighthorse Harry Cooper was a very good player who, like me, just seemed to have certain things happen to him in majors that earned him a reputation of never fulfilling the potential he had. As I did in my escapade at Spring Mill in Philadelphia in 1939 when I miscalculated what I needed to shoot on the final hole, Harry lost the U.S. Open at Oakmont in 1927 by being overly aggressive at the seventy-first hole, thinking he needed a birdie and winding up with a bogey.

He eventually lost to Tommy Armour in the play-off after leading by two. A succession of bad breaks for Harry and Armour's good fortune did him in. Cooper had four good chances to win the Open, and, like yours truly, he managed to botch them.

In the 1938 Canadian Open, I actually was a beneficiary of his misfortune and his loss of concentration. Harry was a very straight hitter—we also used to call him Pipeline—and he rarely made a big mistake like knocking a ball out of bounds. Holding the lead by three on the last hole of the Canadian Open, he waited until an especially rowdy gallery settled down, then promptly went blank and knocked his tee shot over an out-of-bounds fence on the left. He ended up taking a seven for that hole. Coming up behind him, I needed a four to tie, and I had heard what he'd done. I realized I had the whole world to miss it on the right. I hit it so far right it went over the gallery, over a creek and a ditch—so far to the right I couldn't reach the green in two. I laid up to one hundred yards. The pin was cut on the front of the green where I couldn't stop a wedge. The fairway was covered with worm casts, but I played the niftiest little pitch-and-run you ever saw up to about three feet and drained the putt for a tie! I won the play-off, and, on this occasion, I benefited from balls that hit into the gallery and popped back out on the green. Five of them, as I recall. And I think that just wore old Harry out. He was such a high-strung, excitable guy anyway, and he did everything fast. That's why we called him Lighthorse, because he was always on the run. This time, though, he had just run out of steam.

Harry is now ninety-two years old, and though he doesn't play anymore, he still teaches. He lives in Westchester County, New York, and teaches at the Westchester Country Club.

# LIFE ON THE ROAD

Johnny "Boo Boo" Bulla and I were very close during the first few years I played the Tour. We struck up a friendship as soon as we met. You never know why really—why some people you like and some you don't. Johnny was a good man, and we hit it off.

Johnny was brought up a Quaker and had very strong beliefs about how you should treat people. He was a hard worker. Some fellows thought he hit even more balls in practice than Ben Hogan.

We both believed in predestination (but more about that later). Traveling with Johnny in those early days probably helped me handle the successes and the failures. I always looked forward to the quiet times, though there weren't many of those once I started winning regularly. My first year he drove to Tour events, and my second year I drove. After a few years, I decided to drive alone. I wanted to be on my own schedule.

But I always remember what he said about life. He said life is like a three-legged stool with equal parts spiritual, mental, and physical. It can't stand up without solid foundations in each part of your life.

## THE SNEAD SQUAT

I suppose one of the unique parts of my swing that people like to talk about is what's called the Snead Squat. The Snead Squat was the leg action at the very start of my downswing. As I started down, my legs took on a bowing action, with my left leg going toward the target and my right leg seemingly going the opposite way into a squat or a sit-down action. I've seen this position, although maybe not as exaggerated, in some other swings. Some teachers have felt or taught that it was the secret to my swing. A couple of years ago I even had a young professional call me from Dallas and offer to pay me $5,000 to have me teach him the Snead Squat. My son Jackie agreed to have him come to the Greenbrier and spend a couple of days with me, although I didn't charge him a penny.

This position was not something I ever thought about. I wasn't trying to do it. It just happened that way as a result of other moves that were going on in my swing. What I mean is that it was totally unconscious. I was very flexible, and that helped. But I was never trying to hold back my right leg when my knees separated. I did try to pull down with my left side, but I never tried to create this kind of leg action. My focus, if it was on anything—and as I've said, I preferred to think only of rhythm—was on my hands and my arms.

I was never conscious of moving my legs or really even shifting my weight. It came naturally, like walking.

# WE PLAYED TO HAVE FUN, TOO

They say golf is a game of contradictions—swing left, you hit it right. You play to win, but if you can't stand losing, you won't play your best on Sunday. There's a delicate balance that sometimes does seem like a contradiction. A Tour pro can have a nice career nowadays by finishing twenty-fifth in every tournament he plays in. For most of my career, if you finished twenty-fifth, you got nothing! They paid only the top twenty finishers, and even if you won you only got 20 percent of the purse. In the bigger tournaments the purse could be as much as $20,000, which means you made four grand if you won. There were incentives to win, to play your best, but there was another thing that is missing in today's game: fun. We played to have fun, because the Lord knows none of us was getting rich out there!

I like what superagent Mark McCormack said.

He formed the very successful International Management Group (IMG) and represented Arnie, Jack, and Gary Player in the early days. When the Tour started to change into a real money machine, McCormack said that the players should appreciate the opportunities they have and be thankful to all of us old geezers who traveled four to a car, slept two to a bed, and took up every offer of a free dinner from a club member at the host club where we played.

McCormack, who knows a thing or two about money and sports, was ranked as the most powerful man in sports not too long ago by *Sports Illustrated*. He scolded the young fellows on the Tour, saying, "I have a sharp word of sermonizing for the pros of the United States Tour, especially the younger ones. They are getting rich right now on the work of other men, some great ones who, comparatively speaking, never made vast sums from their lifetimes in golf: Walter Hagen, Gene Sarazen, Byron Nelson, Sam Snead, Ben Hogan, Jimmy Demaret. They are the personalities who captivated the public, they made pro golf a successful sport in this country, and they did it when you had a big year if you made ten thousand dollars!"

Most of the fellows in my day enjoyed the company of their fellow players. It was more like a traveling team of ballplayers than the way it is today. The fun didn't end on the course or practice tee, either. It could continue well into the night.

Most of the players found spots to have a drink or two, tell a few stories, and commiserate about missed putts here and there. I wasn't much for drinking, but, like everyone, I did have a good time. I loved the guys out there. Some of my favorites were my old traveling partner Johnny Bulla, Craig Wood, who gave me the push to get out there, Bob Goalby, and Doug Ford. But no one was more fun than Skee Riegel.

Skee was a U.S. Amateur champion and an unbelievable athlete! He had a powerful build and was one of the strongest men I knew. Skee loved to have a few beers with the boys—maybe just a few too many. Eventually, his wife made him stop drinking and focus on his golf.

One time he disobeyed her, however, and I'm afraid his drinking buddies had a lot to do with it. They used to taunt him, saying, "Are you a man or a mouse? Who wears the pants in your house, anyway?" I think it was my old partner, Gardner Dickinson, who challenged him to show off his strength. Skee could walk on his hands, and Dickinson and the boys urged him to show off what he could really do. Pretty soon, Skee was jumping off the bar (on his hands!), hand-walking down a flight of steps, out past the putting green and down the first fairway— with his wife screaming at him every step of the way!

# THE MOST IMPORTANT CLUBS

I have always felt that the order of importance of your clubs is (1) putter, (2) driver, (3) wedge. Most people agree that the putter is the most important club—you use it for more strokes than any other club. You can really help your confidence if you save strokes on the green. The putter can be your best friend or your worst enemy.

I pick the driver as number two because you set up your whole game plan on any hole from where you drive the ball. If you make a bad stroke on a ten-foot putt, well, you just make a good second putt. You *recover.* But sometimes when you drive the ball poorly you can cost yourself more than one stroke. I don't mean driving it out of bounds or in a hazard. If your drive is short or crooked, you may have put yourself in a position that gives you a poor approach to the green.

The wedge is much more important than golfers realize. I think you can save a lot of strokes with good wedge play. I don't mind saying that I was one of the best wedge players. The reason: feel and practice.

I would hit hundreds of wedge shots during my practice sessions. I was trying to get the feel of the swing that hit the ball the yardage I needed to hit it. To this day, if you tell me to hit a wedge fifty-two yards, I feel as if I can do it. It's all feel and touch. I actually hit a lot of balls with my eyes closed, and that helped me to feel the right swing and the right distance.

I never use a sand wedge from the fairway unless I need to hit an unusual shot. I don't like the bounce of a sand wedge. The idea of coming off it a little or knocking it over the green worries me. Why not hit your pitching wedge and feel the distance using your normal swing? The shots I practiced most—fifty-yard, eighty-yard, and one-hundred-yard shots—are your scoring shots.

# HENRY PICARD PICKS ME UP

Henry Picard was a kind of guardian angel to me when I started on the Tour. Henry sold me the driver I used for what seemed like my whole career. Picard was always helping someone out. It was Picard who probably was as responsible as anyone for straightening out Ben Hogan. Hogan dedicated his first instruction book to Picard, for it was Picard who had promised to pay Ben's expenses on the Tour when he was starting out if he couldn't make ends meet.

Henry had spent some time with golf teacher Alex Morrison, who taught him some fundamentals of the swing plane, which Henry then passed on to so many others. Henry believed that a flat swing plane was ideal in all players regardless of their size or physique. He taught people to use proper footwork, rolling the ankles and swinging in balance on a proper plane.

Henry determined that Hogan's swing was too long and that his left-hand grip was too strong—

turned to the right too much. Henry believed you could watch a golfer and see how much he or she could rotate the left wrist and arm and that this counterclockwise motion would tell you where the golfer should place the left-hand grip. It was like magic for Hogan, and the rest, as they say, is history.

Henry's generosity in selling me a driver put me on the right track. He sold it to me for $5.50, which is what he paid for it. I was able to control my shots with this driver. It was heavy, with a very stiff shaft. The story going around that I used it for twenty-three years, that I never let another man hit with it, and that I slept with it was true—except for the last part!

## ALIGNMENT FOR INTENTIONAL HOOKS AND SLICES

On my normal driver swing, I would always drop my right foot back a little, giving me more room to turn and promoting an aggressive inside attack. With this alignment I could play a nice draw and feel a free and easy turn.

If I had to play a hook or a real "coat hanger," as we called it, I would drop my right foot back even more and give the shot more right-to-left spin.

To play a fade, I just opened up by dropping my left foot back a little to cut across the ball a bit.

I didn't really like the idea of changing the swing as such, because that was already grooved or on automatic. I could add spin by adjusting my stance relative to the ball to hit it left-to-right or right-to-left.

This is probably even more important for week-end players than it was for me, because they haven't practiced as much, or grooved their swing as well, so a little adjustment in alignment is actually easier than an adjustment in swing motion.

# A FEEL FOR THE CLUB FACE

I've heard baseball players talk about the fundamental difference between great and good hitters. I'll try to explain it. The great hitters sense where the meat of thc bat is, and they get it on the ball more than average ballplayers. They say it's all a matter of feel. It's a gift from God that they work on to perfcct.

It's the same in golf. You've got to know where that club head is and what's happening to the club face. Some players get the club face on the ball after some strange moves—Miller Barber was one. Yet Miller could get the club face on the ball with the best of them.

I don't agree with the current trend toward lighter club heads, because they take away the feel of where the club face is. I think a heavy-feeling club head is better. My first driver was an E–5 swing weight, and I used it for most of my career. I needed to know where the club face was.

Even as a kid, I remember being concerned with the club face, whether it was open or closed at the top. You can have a pretty swing or one that looks as if it's in all of the right positions, but if you don't have a feel for the club head and club face, you can still hit it sideways.

## LIFE WITH AUDREY

I've wondered what my life would have been like without Audrey. Of course, a man can never really know how much his wife contributes to his success, happiness, or peace of mind. Audrey was definitely a special woman, my first sweetheart and the mother of my two children.

Audrey was very sweet yet very strong-minded. Few people know this, but she was a pretty fair golfer. She won two club championships at our winter home in south Florida and played to about an eight handicap.

Audrey put up with a lot. We had dated through

high school but didn't see much of each other after that until I started out as a professional. Golf was at the center of almost everything we did. We got married in 1940 after I had been around the block a few times. Like many newlyweds in those days, we honeymooned at Niagara Falls. And since the Canadian Open happened to be just a few hours' drive from Niagara Falls, right in the neighborhood you might say, we drove up and I won the tournament. You can imagine the needling I was getting from my fellow players. "Snead's on his honeymoon, he'll be too tired to win this championship!"

Yes, the Tour was different in those days. Audrey traveled with me for our first few years, but after Jackie came along in 1944 it became too hard to concentrate on my work and be a part-time father back at the hotel. Today they have day care for the kids and the travel is easier. So Audrey and Jackie stayed home and I traveled alone. It was the best we knew how to do it at the time. It probably made for better golf, and I certainly slept better without a baby to take care of in the middle of the night, but being away from my family had its costs. It was lonely, and the idea of leaving after the first of the year and not seeing your family until after the Masters in April was not all that appealing. But I did it because I loved the competition and felt I needed to earn more money.

Audrey would often say, "Sam, you've made enough, haven't you?"

And I'd say, "How much is enough?" Times were different, for sure.

Audrey tolerated the fact that I had sowed my wild oats. A single guy could get into a lot of trouble out there. It was easy for the gallery to get up close to you in a tournament back then, and more than once I met my date for that night on the course during my round.

Audrey was a saint, however, taking care of two kids and creating the right kind of home so that we all felt comfortable and secure.

## BUNKER PLAY

Most amateurs are scared to death when they have to blast a ball out of the bunker. It's not such a hard shot, really. Some very simple basics of equipment, setup, and swing apply.

First of all, get yourself a good sand wedge— one with a wide flange on it—one that has bounce. Remember, you're not trying to hit the ball, you're trying to clip some sand out of the bunker. Next to the yip and the shank, the bladed bunker shot is the worst in golf.

Set up with a wider than normal stance. Dig your feet into the sand for a good foundation. Aim a little left, but open the blade of your sand wedge so that it faces the target. Make a nice relaxed but aggressive swing, up and down, and hit two to three inches behind the ball.

Try to remain *very* still in the lower legs during the backswing, and keep most of your weight on the left leg. Don't try to swing outside-in or inside-out, just keep the swing up and down on the same path for the backswing and downswing.

You should take a long, wide, but fairly shallow divot of sand. The two mistakes I see most often from amateurs are lifting up and hitting the equator of the ball, sending it into the next county, or taking a divot of sand large enough to bury a cat!

# THE 1942 PGA
## CHAMPIONSHIP

President Franklin D. Roosevelt had made many speeches about how it might be good for the morale of Americans—both at home and those abroad in the service of their country—if professional baseball and football continued. But many great players had enlisted since competition in sports seemed so relatively unimportant when we were at war. Nevertheless, there was a PGA Tour in spite of gasoline rationing and travel restrictions. I thought about it long and hard and decided to enlist in the navy. Most of the other important players of the era were enlisting. Ben Hogan went into the Army Air Corps, Jimmy Demaret into the navy, and Lloyd Mangrum became an infantryman in the European Theater. Byron Nelson was denied because of a blood-clotting problem.

A lot of people still ask me which championship was my greatest victory, which one filled me with the most pride. Many people expect me to say the 1954 Masters victory over Hogan or my 1946 British Open, but while those championships were good ones to win, my victory in the 1942 PGA is my favorite.

Immediately after Pearl Harbor, the United States declared war, and about six months later, I decided to enlist in the navy. I went down to the navy recruiter in Washington, D.C., and passed my physical, but had one reservation. I wanted a chance to win the PGA Championship, which was being held the next week in Atlantic City, New Jersey. I asked the recruiter if I could delay reporting for duty for a week. He agreed to hold off the signing of the paperwork until after the tournament.

I went on a mission that all of my hardships in previous major championships plus the gloomy prospect of fighting the Germans and Japanese had prepared me for. I had experienced my share of bad luck and had made some foolish mistakes in several major championships. The writers had taken to calling me "The Haunted Hillbilly" and said I was jinxed.

Now remember, the PGA was a match-play tournament in those days. In the final, I faced Jim Turnesa, who was a corporal in the army, stationed at nearby Fort Dix. Turnesa had beaten Byron Nelson and Ben Hogan in order to play me in the final, so I knew I was in for a battle. In addition, about seven thousand unruly army GIs from Fort Dix turned out to root their army buddy on to victory.

For some reason, I was able to block out all of the hostility from Turnesa's gallery. When it was my turn to putt, the gallery would shout, "Miss!" Several times Turnesa's ball would be headed for the rough, only to be kicked back in the fairway.

Going into the final nine holes of our thirty-six-hole match, I was one down, but I could sense that the pressure was getting to Turnesa. All of his mannerisms were changing right before my eyes. He was fiddling with his grip, adjusting it this way and that, on nearly every shot.

One of the ways I learned to adjust my attitude was to hum a victory song, which in this case was "The Merry Widow Waltz." My mind became very clear and quiet, and soon all of my putts were falling. I smelled blood and finished him off with a birdie chip-in from twenty yards on the thirty-fifth hole.

Just that suddenly, the weight of the world was lifted off my shoulders. I had won my first national championship!

When I returned for my induction into the navy, I asked the recruiter if I really could have signed up and postponed my induction. He just laughed at me and said, "Are you kidding? Of course not!"

# MY TAKE ON THE DRIVER SWING

The different lengths of clubs through the set more or less determine the shape of the swing we make with each club. Naturally, your swing with the irons comes up quicker—or is more upright—than with the driver, because the irons are shorter clubs. With the driver, you want to sweep the ball off. But I'll tell you what, I always like to pinch the ball with my driver just a little bit. I feel doing that keeps the swing and the shot on line better. In fact, I want to swing down on the ball with every club. I try to get amateurs to tee the ball low with their driver— barely off the grass—which helps them swing a little down on the ball and pinch it.

I've watched Tiger Woods hit his irons, and he takes a divot of turf that extends eight inches ahead of the ball! That's what I call hitting down on the ball. In my prime, I used to have the longest divots of anybody. You want to hit down and through the ball along the target line.

Back when we had those clinics and long-drive contests for the people before our tournaments, here's what they found when they were out there measuring the distance of our drives. They said that the other players' drives would hit the ground and roll end over end. My drives hit and showed some backspin, but they sure stayed in the air longer and went farther than the others'.

Lee Trevino was nice enough to say that I was the only guy who could hit a driver off a tight downhill lie, and it was because I extended down and through the ball along the line.

Now I'm talking about hitting down on the ball just slightly with the driver because I've already said with its longer shaft, the shape of the swing will be less upright, or flatter, than with the irons.

I've been watching my nephew J. C. Snead, and he drives the ball better now than he ever has. He can throw a ball down there on the grass with no tee and smack it high and straight, as if he had hit it off a tee. It's because he's staying down and through the shot better than before.

# VISUALIZATION AND MENTAL REHEARSAL

One of the most effective tools a golfer can have is the ability to see the shot he wants to hit. I would say that most of the great players in my day visualized naturally. I would use visualization in three ways. Before I got to a tournament, I would picture the course we were going to play, and, especially later in my career, I would imagine the shots that I would fit into the holes. Blueprinting, I called it, and I will discuss it shortly.

The second way I would use visualization was to visualize my swing, especially if there was a problem. I would try to fix it by seeing it better.

The third way I would visualize was to see the shot I wanted to hit—nearly every one. Even today, I get a pretty clear picture in my mind's eye of what a high fade will look like coming into a green, even though I can't see the ball land on the green anymore because of my poor eyesight.

# THE 1946 BRITISH OPEN

The British Open will always give me a special feeling, because one of my proudest moments was winning it in 1946. Of course, some of my most embarrassing moments happened in that British Open as well.

Fact is, I didn't really want to play in the Open. It was just after the war, but Johnny Bulla talked me into it. Johnny and I were like brothers—we fought all the time! He told me I needed to play in the British Open at St. Andrews because it was the home of golf. "You've just got to, Sam."

My first impressions of St. Andrews weren't so good. And, man, did I ever get myself into trouble! As we rode the train into St. Andrews, I looked out at the countryside, which appeared to be just an empty field. A fence was torn down here, the grass was overgrown there, and there were some sandy bunkers that looked pretty unkempt.

I said to a fella sitting next to me, "What abandoned golf course is that?" Well, you would have thought I'd said something unflattering about his sister!

He sat bolt upright. "I'll have you know that is St. Andrews, sir!"

Not impressed, I said, "Is *that* where they're going to hold the British Open?"

The Open Championship they called it, and, frankly, I didn't much care for their attitude about it. I would get myself in even more trouble with my mouth later. After my first round, some reporters asked me what I thought of St. Andrews. I said I was disappointed. Well, you would have thought I had dragged the Royal Family through the Road Hole bunker by their ankles!

And Bulla tells me I need to play the British Open at the home of golf where Jones, Hagen, Sarazen, Vardon, Ray, and others had played. Bulla disappeared on me. He wouldn't play a practice round with me, he wouldn't eat with me, and he wouldn't even talk to me.

Maybe I embarrassed him. Maybe he thought I was the man to beat and didn't want me to get too comfortable. I think Bulla thought, If I beat Snead I can win the British Open. We were paired together in one round, and he was beating me by three shots by the time we reached the Road Hole, the seventeenth. This hole is a long one, where so many Opens have been won or lost. At the time, if you

85

were a long hitter like me you just aimed it out of bounds over some coal sheds—now it's the Old Course Hotel—and busted it.

Well, I launched it over the sheds and had only a six iron onto the green, which is one of the more interesting greens in the world. That hole has a cobblestone road to the right and back of the green and a wall behind that. The greens were hard and fast—they must have had roots about two feet deep!

Bulla took a three iron and tried to hit a rope hook into the green. Well, it was a crazy shot to play, because even if he hit the green it would have gone over onto the road. As it was, he hit it left.

I played a smart shot—one that I had blueprinted earlier. Instead of hitting the six iron I hit a four iron along the ground just in front of the green. There was no way I was going to get that ball up into the wind and risk going into the Road Bunker—or worse, over the back onto the road. In my blueprint I knew I could make a par from just in front of the green, and I did. Meanwhile, Bulla was on the road. You would have thought it was the Fourth of July the way the sparks flew when his club collided with the road. He made seven.

The sparks flew again on the eighteenth tee when Johnny said, "Well, I guess you're satisfied now. You're tied with me."

I said, "John, you just played a dumb second shot."

I learned a lot in the 1946 Open Championship. It was one of my proudest moments to win that silver claret jug. I learned how much respect the British have for the game of golf, for its traditions, and its champions. I learned a little more about myself—maybe there are some things I wouldn't say today—and I learned about how to compete, how to win the battle within yourself. I learned that you should plan to play a golf course. Sure, I had heard this wisdom before and I had watched great champions like Walter Hagen use this approach, but never until the 1946 British Open did I recognize the importance of having a plan to play a course, a blueprint.

## BLUEPRINTING

I wish I had learned to blueprint my rounds earlier in my career. I am sure I would have won many more tournaments, especially the U.S. Opens I lost. If I had shot sixty-nines in my final rounds in the U.S.

Open, I would have won nine times! Bad thinking cost me dearly, but more on my battles with the U.S. Open later.

I think the average amateur golfer can learn a lot from the mistakes I made and save himself some strokes—not to say a few bucks, too—if he follows a few rules of blueprinting:

1. The first thing is to know your game completely. Know what shots you can play and which ones you can't. Most amateurs take needless risks. They try to hit the perfect shot every time, forgetting too easily that they wouldn't be in the trouble they're in if they hadn't topped their drive into the hazard in front of the tee!
2. Sometimes amateurs should deliberately play short of bunkers or hazards. Even Ben Hogan, Walter Hagen, and I did that!
3. Walter Hagen once told me that while planning a shot he would always ask himself what his margin for error was. Only when he had convinced himself that his chances were better than fifty-fifty did he try a risky shot. And they called Hagen a riverboat gambler! It seems to me that Hagen was a master of himself and that he succeeded because he only tried to hit shots he knew he could bring off.

The key to understanding your game is taking a good clear look at the way you have been playing.

What clubs, what part of your game gives you the most trouble? Do you start well, get frustrated, and lose your concentration? Do you start poorly because you're not warmed up or too nervous?

Once you really come to know yourself, your tendencies, and your swing, you can follow the rest of my blueprinting plan of attack. But until you really know what you *can do* (and what you *can't*) you won't ever become the kind of player you want to be.

The other step in blueprinting is to understand the course and the conditions you might face. You should plan out where you want to hit *each shot*. *Place* every shot to a target that you can hit—not one in ten times but maybe eight in ten times. Visualize both the course and your swing on each of these blueprinted shots. Play for a position—not for a score. You'll feel a lot more confidence if you're executing the shots you've planned out in your game plan.

I have played a lot of golf with champions from other sports (more on this later), and I know that this is a secret that is shared by all great athletes. In baseball a pitcher knows which pitches he can throw and which ones he can't. He doesn't try to throw a knuckleball that isn't part of his repertoire—no matter how big the game. He studies the opposition hitters and tries to match his strengths with the hitter's weaknesses. He plays for position. He has a conservative strategy. If a guy's a dead fastball hitter, a pitcher isn't fool enough to try a fastball down the middle to him.

# MENTAL MATURITY

I won a lot of golf tournaments by just letting it fly. I lost more tournaments by being too bold. After I'd been around awhile and observed how Walter Hagen, Gene Sarazen, and Henry Cotton played the game, I learned how to fit my shots into a hole.

By 1949, I had begun to tell myself to place my drive. I'd hit a little draw on this hole, a little fade on the next—just to keep my ball in play. Now, on a par five, if there was no trouble, I'd bust it off the tee. I knew I could reach the green in two if I hit it hard. But with water on the right, or an out-of-bounds on the left, I would tell myself to play it smart— lay up. I'd pitch my third shot on, and I'd make birdie more than half the time. And I stayed away from those nasty sixes and sevens! That's what eats you up inside. In 1950, I played ninety-six rounds—twenty-four tournaments—and averaged 69.2 strokes per round, so my thinking paid off. I won eleven tournaments in 1950 and earned $35,000. I hate to think what winning eleven tournaments in 1997 would bring—too many millions.

# DIEGELING WITH LEO

I never had a formal lesson in golf, but believe me, I was always on the lookout for ways to improve my mental game. Most veteran players were in my day—they would try to learn something from the fellows who were racking up all the tournament victories.

Leo Diegel was one of the best players around in the 1920s and '30s, but he had trouble getting relaxed enough to be able to win the big ones. Leo was such a jumpy guy he had to invent a new kind of putting stroke in order to keep from breaking down at impact. When Leo addressed the ball, he looked like a chicken about to fly. His hold on the putter featured elbows locked in a chicken-wing fashion and pointed parallel to the target line. He bent way down over the ball and locked his wrists, arms, and hands into a triangle. In fact, "Diegeling" was a term at the time that referred to Leo's putting style. He won two PGA championships, back-to-back, '28 and '29, so he conquered the battle of nerves, but he had lost earlier wars with his emotions.

Leo was the victim of Walter Hagen's gamesmanship on more than one occasion, but the way it ended up for him he was able to learn from his mistakes, conquer his nerves, and pass on some wisdom to me on how to exercise better self-control.

In a PGA Championship in the late 1920s, Leo was one up on Walter Hagen going to the thirty-fifth hole of their match. Leo had driven into the fairway, and Hagen had hit a bad hook into the left trees. Leo thought Walter was in bad shape, until Hagen took out his brassie, or two wood, waggling it and looking for all intents and purposes as if he had a clear shot to the green. Leo changed his strategy and decided to hit his own brassie, but then hit a poor shot into the front bunker.

Hagen walked slowly back to his bag, took an iron and pitched out of the trees onto the fairway, knocked it stiff on his third shot, and made par. Leo hit a poor bunker shot and two-putted for a bogey to lose the hole. Still steaming from his mental error,

Leo lost the thirty-sixth hole and the match to Sir Walter. The lesson was clear enough—take responsibility for your own ball and your own score—the only ones you have control over.

Leo made a study of Hagen and his mental game and passed it on to me. Hagen had dominated the PGA Championship in the twenties, winning five of them, including four in a row, leading up to the 1928 PGA. Remember, the PGA was a match-play elimination tournament then. The 1928 quarter-finals featured—you guessed it—Walter Hagen and Leo Diegel. Up until this time, Sir Walter was thought to be nearly unbeatable. His mental management was far superior to any of the players of his day. But Leo had a plan.

Diegel told me that it bothered him that Walter was such a slow and deliberate player. He took such a long time to choose his shots. This drove Leo crazy, but he said that if he could exercise enough self-control to walk *behind* Hagen onto the green, he could slow himself down enough to be able to beat him. And sure enough, Leo tried never to enter the green in front of Walter and pulled off one of the greatest upsets of the day by beating Hagen two and one. He then steamrollered over Gene Sarazen in the semifinals seven and six, and whipped Al Espinosa six and five in the finals.

# THE RELAXATION RESPONSE

Your system to playing and learning golf should be to keep it as simple and natural as possible. Your system should be one that enables you to relax and to attain a mastery over yourself. The difference between great athletes and ordinary ones, I believe, is that great athletes are able to recognize tension and pressure, to control it and to thrive on it.

Don't be afraid to take your game very seriously—try to improve always—but don't allow the need to play your best build up so much tension that you can't play naturally and easily.

I used a few tricks on the course under tournament pressure, and the boys I played against had some of their own.

After my son Jackie was born, I would relax myself on the course by thinking about him and how simple the game must seem in his eyes. I recall one particular tournament in which he and Audrey were watching me in an especially tense situation. He asked her if I was going to win the tournament, and she told him that if I sank the next putt I would win. He told her that he was hungry and that he wanted me to hurry up and make it. Fortunately, I did, but I recalled the experience many times to remind myself that *we make ourselves tense* by the thoughts we have and it probably does no good to remind ourselves of the "pressure" we feel to hole the next putt.

# THE KILLER INSTINCT

Growing up, I played a lot of baseball, football, and basketball, and I ran track. I even tried my hand at prizefighting. There was competition every day at something. You learned to develop your killer instinct. We appreciated athletes in other sports who had trained themselves to be mentally tough.

The great heavyweight champion Joe Louis was a friend of mine and developed into quite a good golfer. He even played in a Tour event or two.

He would always admire how solid I could hit

the ball and how long I would drive it. Playing with me he would always try to reach back for something extra. In one round we played together in San Diego, he hit an awful snap hook that hit a guy in a place you don't want to be hit. The guy took two steps and went down as if he'd been shot. Although the poor guy was in pain, it sure was funny in a cartoonish kind of way when you saw him from the tee.

Sugar Ray Robinson was also a friend of mine and a decent player. Sugar Ray wanted to challenge me in golf and in boxing using a handicap system. In golf, he wanted me to give him a stroke a hole, which I think I could have handled, but what he proposed in boxing didn't fit my instinct as a gambler. He said he'd spot me five rounds in a six-round fight. I said, "That's fine, as long as I can use my wedge."

That's another reason why I love golf and think it's the greatest game. People of different abilities can play together and have a good time doing it.

# JIMMY DEMARET

Jimmy Demaret was called "The Ambassador of Golf" because he was not only a very good player (he won the Masters in 1940, 1947, and 1950) but because he was a goodwill ambassador for the sport. Jimmy was known for his colorful wardrobe. In fact, up until Demaret began wearing colors other than gray, black, and white, you didn't see much in the way of colors on a professional golfer.

Jimmy was a funny man, a friend to all. I think Hogan admired Demaret in many ways, and they became friends. Jimmy even wrote a book called *Ben Hogan, My Partner,* although I don't think it revealed anything about Hogan since even with Demaret Ben was very guarded.

Hogan admired the way Demaret hit the ball— quail-high, and with a fade. Hogan would have sold his soul to Satan himself if he could have had that shot in the thirties and early forties!

Hogan also admired the way Jimmy handled

people. Jimmy could hold court with the best of them. He and Jack Burke, Jr., built and developed the Champions Golf Club in Houston, which featured two long, hard golf courses and a men's grillroom where every day Jimmy (and now, Jackie, Jr.) would hold court.

Jimmy will always be known as one of the first ad-lib color commentators on TV. The guy did everything with such apparent ease. I thought it was amazing that he could win three Masters green jackets hitting that high fade at Augusta National. Two other things amazed me—he never seemed to practice, and he never seemed to sleep.

The last time he won at Augusta, in 1950, I remember players saying that he closed down the bar in the old Bon Air Hotel after having a few and singing with the band. This was Saturday night before the final round, and there were odds that he wouldn't make it out of bed in the morning—but he won the championship just the same.

He was such a friendly fellow people would write him for advice, and he loved giving amateurs tips on their game. One fellow wrote to him and said, "Jimmy, I'm busting my driver down the middle on every hole and I'm hitting my three wood 245 yards with about an eight-yard fade. What should I do?"

Jimmy wrote back: "Turn pro."

# BREATHING AND HEART RATE

You hear a lot these days about things like breathing and how it can influence the way you swing or stroke a putt. It's as if somebody just invented breathing! Sure, breathing is important, and in my day we knew a little bit about it.

Bobby Jones used to tell the story of how he'd get all pumped up during match play in the U.S. Amateur, and, even though he had won the U.S. Open, he hadn't managed to win the U.S. Amateur yet. He discovered that when he reached the green his heart rate was much too fast and his breathing was all fouled up. By focusing on slowing down his heart and breathing well before he putted, he was able to climb down to a level where he could putt better. Sure enough, he would win the 1924 U.S. Amateur at Merion by focusing on his breathing on the greens!

Byron Nelson was also a master at sensing when his breathing and heart rate were out of sync. Byron made it a fundamental not to walk too fast, because he knew his breathing would get fast and that his heart rate would go up and that the whole rhythm of his swing would change. When you watched Byron play he always looked like a cow out for a stroll.

I was aware of my breathing, and, when it got shallow and fast, I knew I needed to slow down. The more you are in tune with your thinking and with what your body is doing, the better you are able to control your swing. This sensitivity that I had to what I was feeling and thinking helped me perform better. I'm sure of it.

The first time I was really aware of the critical importance of breathing was while I was running the one-hundred-yard sprint. I knew I could consistently run around ten seconds flat, which was good in my day, though now both the boys and the girls can fly! When my breathing was right, I would take two breaths in the one hundred and two breaths only. It helped my body and mind work together better.

---

*Byron Nelson on Sam*

---

Sam Snead is a great credit to the game of golf. I don't think anyone in the world has ever played as well as Sam for as long a period of time.

Sam was very relaxed on the golf course. He would never give the appearance of being very serious on the course—unless, of course, he was trying to win a tournament. He would tell jokes and always try to have a good time. I know he was deadly serious about winning, though you could hardly tell.

Sam was like a cat. His coordination and his movements were so athletic, so different from most players'. When I would be playing with Sam he would surprise you with the things he could do. We would walk off a tee, and if there was a bench there he'd hop over it just like a rabbit!

People often compare Snead, Hogan, and me because we played together so much. Certainly both Snead and Hogan were absolutely marvelous players. We were completely different person- alities, especially the way we concentrated. Sam could go out very relaxed and play just shot for shot. He would try to do the best he could on every shot, and I think I was the same way. We didn't much care about shooting a score. We wanted to perform the best we could possibly per- form, and, if we didn't beat the other man, well that was okay. Sam never gave any thought, nor did I, about what he needed to shoot to win.

Ben was the exact opposite. He had a great power of concentration, but if his concentration got broken, he'd take a long time to get it back. That was why he was so quiet on the golf course. He was trying to get into the zone, so to speak, and when he got out of it—why, he couldn't get back into it very well.

Ben had a great ability to figure out what score it might take to win. He would try to shoot that score, and if he won it was okay and if he lost it was what he wanted to shoot. I think that's why Ben's play-off record was so poor. He'd already set his goal for what he'd shoot, and it let him down many times. Both Sam and I got the better of Ben, and maybe this was why.

Snead hated losing. So did Ben, and so did I. The main thing we had in common, I feel, is we wanted to play the very best we could play. We did not want to get beat. It wasn't that we hated anybody, but we were very competitive. We wanted to win!

---

# LORD BYRON

In 1945, Byron Nelson won eleven consecutive PGA tournaments and a total of eighteen for the year. It's one of the most remarkable streaks in the history of sports. The only streak of its kind that's comparable is Joe DiMaggio's fifty-six-game hitting streak in baseball.

Byron is the senior member of the threesome of

Nelson, Hogan, and Snead. Byron was born on the fourth of February 1912. He lived in a small town outside of Fort Worth, Texas, and as everyone now knows he learned to play golf the way we all did back then—by caddying. One of his fellow caddies was none other than little Ben Hogan, at the Glen Garden Club in Fort Worth.

Byron grew up in a very strict family. His father was a country farmer and, like my father, a hard worker, very quiet, and without especially good business instincts. His mother was a bit like my mother, also very much in control of what went on at home. Byron used to say that his parents demanded respect. He knew they loved him, but he also knew he needed to toe the line. To this day, Byron will tell you that what he is proudest of is that he is remembered as a gentleman, as "a person who lived right and did right."

Growing up, Byron played caddie tournaments and city championships and the like. He was the kid to beat, and I don't think Ben Hogan ever got the best of him. Byron says that even as a kid, he never got to know Ben. Ben was different from the other fellows, a scrapper, a fighter.

Over the span of what would be a relatively short career, Byron won fifty-two events, starting with the 1935 New Jersey Open and ending with the 1951 Crosby. Byron actually left the Tour after the 1946 season, but he played an occasional event after that.

103

Byron was a remarkable guy. What people don't realize today is that most of us on the Tour in those days also had club jobs, and Byron was no exception.

Byron's motivation for playing the Tour was a little different from Ben's and mine. He wanted to win as much as anyone, but he also wanted to provide for his family—to win money to support his parents and, later, his wife, Louise, and himself. The first thing he did when he'd won enough money was buy his parents a big ranch near Denton, Texas, and set his father up in business. His idea of the good life seemed to be to have a big ranch with lots of cattle, chickens, and horses and to make sure that his family was safe and secure. That was his dream, and he lived it. Who can criticize that? To this day, he's a happy fellow, very much involved in his ranching, his church activities, his tournament—the Byron Nelson Classic—and its charities. He accomplished all of his goals, and not many people can say that.

During his streak year of 1945, Byron was magical. He couldn't seem to play a bad round. The pressure was amazing, but Byron handled it with his usual grace. His approach was interesting. He had grooved his swing and was pretty happy with it, so during the streak he stopped practicing. He would arrive at the course, warm up a bit, hit out a dozen balls, hit a few putts to get comfortable with the speed of the greens, and then go shoot sixty-five! Of course, Hogan would rather practice than play, so this was heresy to him and some others.

There were a lot of misconceptions about the streak and about Byron, just as there were about Ben and me. Some said Byron didn't have the stomach for the competition. Nothing could have been further from the truth. Byron was a fighter—he just enjoyed other things more than Tour life.

Even today I hear people say Byron competed against weak fields—the war just having ended and many of us still doing our military service. Byron was rejected for military service because of a blood-clotting problem, but he still served his country by doing exhibitions for the Red Cross and the USO— over a hundred, I think. Just because he didn't wear a uniform like Ben and I did didn't mean he didn't do his service. Remember now, I was in San Diego giving golf lessons and designing golf courses for the navy, and Ben was doing much the same with the Army Air Corps.

About the weak fields: Byron competed against me, Hogan, Jimmy Demaret, Lloyd Mangrum, Jug McSpaden, Ralph Guldahl, Sam Byrd, and other great players. I played twenty-eight events in 1945, and I finished first in six. Of course, Ben wouldn't really come into his own until 1946, but he still won five events and played in thirteen others.

My view of Byron's career is that it was a bit like Bobby Jones's. Jones won the Grand Slam (or the Impregnable Quadrilateral, as it was then called, and boy, I'm sure glad they changed it). And then he called it quits. There were no other worlds to conquer. Or there *were* worlds to conquer—they just were different from the ones the sportswriters thought worthy. We shouldn't be forced to chase someone else's dream or even someone else's idea of what is good enough.

Byron had decided that once he had won all of the important tournaments in the United States and once he had enough money to support Louise and himself, he'd become a rancher. And he did. Of course, he did design some courses, did do television color commentary, and played in an occasional event. He helped a number of younger players along the way as well, although he wasn't really known as a teacher of golf. Ken Venturi and Tom Watson were both schooled by him, and each went on to become major championship winners.

Incidentally, Byron and I made some of the same mistakes when we were younger. Neither of us smoked cigarettes or drank alcohol, but many of the sponsors of our tournaments were tobacco or beer companies. Both Byron and I accepted money to appear in advertising for tobacco companies. Of course, money was short in the 1930s, so we both did it.

A tobacco company gave Byron the then huge sum of $500 to endorse its cigarettes, and Byron agreed. When Byron started getting letters from

Sunday school teachers asking "How could you?" he got very upset at his decision. He called the company and said he would give all of the money back, but the executives refused and the ads kept appearing. Poor Byron was so distraught. You wish the athletes of today would have a little of Byron's role-model sense of responsibility.

I think the thing with Byron was that he was a happy man. When he wanted to go out on the Tour, his father and mother didn't think much of the idea. But they changed their minds when they saw how much he wanted to do it. They gave him their blessing and said, "You've always been a good boy. Just go out there and give it your best shot." And he made them very proud.

## In the Zone

Most golfers never say much about the mental part of their game. Athletes don't enjoy talking about what is going on in their minds. The reasons for this are many. Why would you want to give away your secrets to everyone else? Why would you want to give up your edge over another player by giving him hints as to how you conquered a particular challenge? I hated it when people asked me to talk about my mind-set, perhaps as much as I hated losing at anything I did. I think a great athlete will always leave a little unsaid.

Another reason is that the self-consciousness that comes with revealing your approach could be detrimental to keeping that approach. The example I give you is what people call the zone now. I had never heard about this thing called the zone. In my day, we had a term called the trance, which I think means the same thing. Even back then, though, we didn't talk about it much—maybe it was superstition or the thought that it would go away if you talked about it. You'd come off the course and you'd hear, "Nelson shot a sixty-four today, nothing affected him, he looked like he was walking around in a trance."

I'm not exactly sure how it happens—it just does. When you're in the zone you feel more relaxed. Everything feels smooth. Your senses become sharper. You see all things more clearly. You can see the line of every putt. Your visualization is very clear.

Your whole feel is different in the zone. Your touch seems different: It's lighter, it's smoother, it's easier. You're more relaxed. You don't think about anything but the shot you need to hit, and you think you can hit any shot you need to. It doesn't make a difference if it's a shot you had a problem with yesterday, now it flows. You're not trying to hit the shot, you just do it. And there are no mechanics—heavens, no, there's nothing to think about. There's work to do, and you just do it and go to the next shot. You never feel as if you can't do what your mind is telling you to do.

Yes, the zone is very much something that just happens, but the more you try to make it happen the farther away it gets. That made a lot of us superstitious about the mental game.

Whenever I was asked about it, I always said, "I'm not there yet."

I think some players today are too mechanical. They're trying to get in this or that position. It's got to be harder to get in the zone if you're worried about your mechanics. You have to feel free and easy. And now that you have an idea of what it feels like, if it happens to you, you can just ride along with it and enjoy it.

# BANTAM BEN HOGAN

The late Ben Hogan was born on August 13, 1912, also in a small town near Fort Worth, Texas. Like Byron Nelson and myself, he was born into a poor family. Chester Hogan, Ben's dad, did various odd jobs, including working in a Dr Pepper plant and smithing. Ben had a brother and sister, and after Ben's dad committed suicide when Ben was six, Ben's mom became a seamstress. Ben earned his way through his childhood selling newspapers and doing odd jobs.

Ben was a tough little guy who learned to fend for himself and maybe by the sheer force of his will made himself a success. Heaven knows, there was very little in his young life that would make you want to think he would later become one of the greatest golfers in the history of the game.

Ben was a mystery to me. He could be cordial and poised, but as I say, he gave away less of himself than any man I've ever known.

Ben boxed and dealt cards but quickly found out what he really enjoyed: hitting golf balls. As a caddie at Glen Garden he was not held in the kind of esteem that Byron Nelson was and, quite clearly, was not in Byron's league as a player. In spite of the fact that he really showed little promise, he turned professional in 1931 and headed out to try the Tour. Three times he returned to Fort Worth because he had run out of money, but each time he went back. There was no beating Ben Hogan.

He finally won an event, the North and South Open at Pinehurst in 1940, nine years after starting out. He would go on to win sixty-three tournaments, third on the all-time PGA victory list. He would win every major championship and set new standards for ball-striking excellence.

Ben was troubled early in his career by the dreaded duck hook. He had a long swing and a strong grip, and he could have bouts of the hooks that would kill an ordinary man.

Over a period of a few years, Ben weakened his grip, shortened his swing, and, as often as not, began playing a slight fade—like his partner, Jimmy Demaret. Ben was, until late in his competitive career, one of the best putters we had on tour. He was marvelous around the greens.

Ben came into his own just as Byron Nelson left the Tour, so if there was any competition between the two, and many people believed there was, Byron got the better of Ben.

One of the most obvious differences between Ben and Byron and me was in the manner we handled mistakes. Ben, Byron, and I were all fierce competitors—none of us liked losing. Byron seemed to accept that he was human and that he would miss a shot here or there. And I think I was much the same way. You got the feeling that Ben hated, I mean hated, the mistakes he made. The manner in which he talked about his performance when it was poor was so angry and unforgiving that you found yourself feeling sorry for him.

I think the first time I ever saw Ben Hogan was in 1938 at the Oakland Open. His car had just been vandalized, the tires stolen, and he was wailing and hitting a brick wall.

Ben was a clever businessman, unlike Byron and me. The stories are now legendary. A photographer would ask permission to take Hogan's picture swinging a club, and Hogan would ask what the photographer had paid Snead to have *his* picture taken. Hogan would then demand two or three times the fee I had gotten.

Ben was known to be terse and cold if he didn't like you or didn't have the time for you. Gary Player swears by his story about asking Hogan for advice. Ben said, "What brand of clubs do you play with, may I ask?"

Player said, "Dunlop."

Hogan said, "Then you can call Mr. Dunlop and ask him." And he hung up!

Ben could be very gentle and courteous, especially to women. While shy, he was very well spoken. He was for all practical purposes about as opposite a person as one could be from Jimmy Demaret, who welcomed the younger players on tour and was very free with advice. John Mahaffey, who would go on to win many Tour events and a PGA Championship, asked Hogan's advice about how to become a better player. Hogan barked, "You have a shag bag?"

Mahaffey said, "Yes, sir."

Hogan's response was "Then use it!"

## BEN HOGAN, BYRON NELSON, AND ME

Ben, Byron, and I each accomplished a little bit in our careers and were probably as different as three players could be in our approaches.

If you asked Hogan almost anything about his game, he didn't have an answer. He sort of snorted. He didn't want to give up any of his edge. He didn't want you knowing what he thought about. The guy rarely said anything to anyone about anything. Frankly, I am suspicious of anyone who says he was Hogan's friend or that he knew a lot about Ben.

I was as close to Ben as about anyone on the Tour, and I never felt I got to know him. Don't get me wrong, Ben was a fine man, a gentleman and maybe the best player ever. You just couldn't get to know him, and that's the way he wanted it.

He sure was a strange little guy, though. Everyone thought we didn't get along, but I never had any problem with Ben. He played his game, and I played mine. Once we represented the United States in the Canada Cup (now called the World Cup) in Great Britain. He wouldn't even ride in the same car as me going out to the course. But I think he was just getting himself ready to play, and I respected that. He never said much on the course, except "You're away."

We played some exhibitions in the Pacific Northwest and had to stay in the same room. That's when I learned that he ground his teeth. Sometimes the sound was so loud I couldn't sleep, so I'd kick the bed and say, "Ben, turn over, turn over." When I told Jimmy Demaret about Ben's grunting and grinding his teeth, Demaret said, "He's sharpening his blue-blades for the next day!"

Something that might surprise people is that I never watched Ben hit a shot during a tournament. Ben had a very quick tempo, and I learned early in my career never to watch someone whose tempo was different from mine. Ben was just too fast. About the only player I enjoyed watching while I was playing in a tournament was Jim Turnesa. He had a fine swing and wonderful tempo.

Byron tells one on me. I used to give him the needle about his approach. Byron was a great fellow and a great player. After a few years on the Tour, Byron stopped practicing, and in his best years he'd show up, hit twenty balls, and go out and shoot sixty-six. While he was always polite, friendly, and professional he didn't seem to be having much fun, and I said as much. He told some people, "Tell Snead I had a lot of fun winning all those tournaments." Winning is fun, he was right.

I used humor to relax me and to have fun. Byron's approach was different from mine, and, of course, Ben's was a different game altogether. His response to people who asked him if he had fun and why he never seemed to smile on the course was "There's nothing funny out there!"

I think Ben learned from his earlier career when breaks in his concentration cost him. So he taught himself just to look down and block out all that was going on around him. He'd hardly ever say a word while you were playing with him. And that was just Ben Hogan's way of playing. He would say, "Well, I can't concentrate on playin' if I say, 'Hello, Joe, how ya doin'? How's Mary? How are the kids?' I can't do that. I just want to concentrate on what I'm doing, I don't want to talk."

The best story about Hogan's concentration is from the 1948 Masters. He was playing with Claude Harmon. They were playing the twelfth hole. Claude made a hole in one. Ben made a two. As they were walking to the next tee, the Hawk said, "That's the first time I've ever made a two there. What did you have, Claude?"

"Why, I had a hole in one, Ben."

Another version I've heard is that Hogan said, "I never hit that green" (after going over the green). "What did you make there, Claude?"

Both stories are good fun and contribute to the Hogan legend. But neither one is true. Hogan was interviewed after the round and described Harmon's ace.

A story that I know happened the way the legend has it concerns how Ben helped Claude concentrate better, which almost won him a U.S. Open. Claude was the pro down at the Seminole Golf Club in North Palm Beach, Florida, where Hogan loved to

116

play and practice. The shots—especially the ones into the fast-sloping greens—reminded him of the ones he'd have to face at Augusta National in the Masters. Claude was also the pro at Winged Foot in New York, where the 1959 U.S. Open was held.

They sure had fixed up old Winged Foot for the Open. It was a brutal test of golf. The course was long and hard. The rough was high. The bunkers around the Tillinghast greens were treacherous. The greens were diabolical and lightning-fast. Billy Casper won the tournament with a two over par, and, man, that guy could putt his ball!

Ben and Claude played practice rounds together. Ben told Claude that if he wanted to play well he'd have to pay more attention to his game and less to his membership. Ben said, "Claude, when you get to that first tee: Head down. Don't look up. When they call you to the tee, you go on up, hit the ball, and you just go on down that fairway right to your ball. You don't see anybody on the sidelines, in the gallery."

Apparently, Claude thought he could handle that, but he was really worried about the long walk between nine and ten. The walk from the ninth green to the tenth tee at Winged Foot goes right in front of the clubhouse, where the members have lunch. Claude said to Ben, "But, Ben, how 'bout the ninth hole and my members?"

Ben said, "You don't even hear 'em. You just

keep goin'. They'll adjust and say, 'Hey, he don't want to be bothered. He just wants to play his game.'" Well, Claude finished second in that U.S. Open—his best finish ever in an Open—so I guess Hogan was right.

# CONCENTRATION: THE KEY TO SUCCESS

I have always felt that you could have all the talent in the world but if you can't focus you won't come anywhere near achieving your potential in golf. Once you get on the course, *it's all concentration.*

My approach to concentration was to try to focus only on what was happening at the moment. I played shot to shot, one shot at a time. I didn't try to stay focused for the entire round.

I think you stay on an even keel better if you just focus on each shot. After I hit a shot, if I liked how I did it, I just let it go. If I didn't like it, I said to myself, "Now, why did I do that?"

One of the things I did pretty well was visualize the shot I wanted to play. By seeing that shot, I didn't get all tied up in swing thoughts or what Jimmy Demaret might have made on the last hole. I knew that I had practiced every possible shot, so I didn't need to worry about *whether* I could hit it. I would see the ball in the air—maybe I'd be playing a high cut—the ball fading in there. I would see it all the way. And then my body would take over and hit the shot.

## BEATING HOGAN AT RIVIERA

One of the most inspirational comebacks in the history of sports was Ben Hogan's emotional return to the Tour after he nearly died when a Greyhound bus collided with his car on a foggy highway in West Texas. Ben's rehabilitation looked hopeless at times, but that little fellow was a tough character! He made his triumphant return in January of 1950, twelve months after nearly dying.

I'm only a footnote in the Ben Hogan comeback story, but I was fortunate (or unfortunate) enough to be the guy who beat him in a play-off for the 1950 L.A. Open title at Riviera in his first appearance back on the Tour.

Playing with bandages on his legs, Ben shot a final round of sixty-nine to go with a seventy-three in the first round and sixty-nines in the second and third rounds. I was on the back nine when the club-house celebration started. This was the greatest comeback in the history of sports, and the party was on!

I needed to figure out how to birdie five of the last seven holes in order to tie Hogan. Up until that point my putting had not been good, but I had to make it work. Well, I birdied twelve and thirteen, parred fourteen, birdied fifteen, parred sixteen, and birdied seventeen, just as I pictured in my mind's eye. Now I had to make a three at the difficult eighteenth in order to be the party pooper.

I had to make a fifteen-foot putt on the final hole of regulation in order to tie Hogan. Riviera's greens are diabolical, and I recall looking over the putt for quite some time. One sportswriter said I took three minutes to line it up! All I know is I was pretty tight. Just before I stroked the putt, a funny thing happened that might have enabled me to make it.

Riviera's eighteenth hole is a natural amphi-theater and one of the greatest places to watch the action in all of golf. There's always a lot of commotion around that particular green, as it sits below the clubhouse. Just as I was feeling that my brain was about to explode with all the tension I had allowed to build up, a spectator fell out of a tree! I'm sure it was embarrassing and painful to the poor guy who fell, but for me it was just the break in the tension I needed. I rolled that fifteen-footer right into the cup to tie The Hawk.

The play-off wasn't held until the next week, not the next day, as was usually the case in the days before sudden-death play-offs. Rain had made Riviera unplayable, and there was the Crosby to play up the coast in Monterey. So when it finally happened, the play-off was a bit of a disappointment to Ben's adoring fans, as I shot seventy-two to Ben's seventy-six. It was anticlimactic and would have made a better story if Ben had beaten me.

# 1950: SWEET AND BITTER

Nineteen fifty was my best year. I won eleven tournaments and played ninety-six rounds with an average 69.23 strokes, which won me the Vardon Trophy for the lowest average per round. That was also the year I beat Ben Hogan in the play-off at Riviera in the L.A. Open.

I was the leading money winner that year as well as in 1949, and I realized a couple of important things about my game. At the start of the year, I said to myself, "I'm not going to try to outdrive everybody, or anybody, but I'm going to play the golf course. If it needs a little cut, why, I'll cut it. If it needs a little hook, I'll hook it." I found out that the more I stayed in the fairway, the more chances I had for birdie. That's when I decided to play with about 85 percent of my power.

When I would come to a par five, I would let out the shaft a little bit, but I realized that I couldn't do that on every shot. You have got to stay back where you can swing the club with poise and balance. The minute you start to try to hit the ball as hard as you can on every shot, then you're going to hit a lot of balls on the heel and toe of the club and miss a lot of shots. I carried all of this over into 1950 and through the rest of my career.

Ben Hogan won two tournaments in 1950, the Greenbrier and the U.S. Open, and was named "Golfer of the Year" by the PGA. I almost quit the Tour after that, and I did cut back on the number of tournaments I played from then on. It was like this. The PGA said, "Snead won the trophy for Best Player in '49, let's give it to Ben this year."

I said, "Hey, that's not right. I won eleven tournaments; that's the best I've ever done." I kind of lost a little of my desire to go out and play after that.

Of course, 1950 was Ben's comeback year after his near fatal car accident. It was called the "greatest comeback in sports history," and I won't argue with that. Heck, they could have given him a six-foot trophy as the best comeback kid, but he just wasn't the best player that year.

After that I said, "The hell with it," and cut back on my playing significantly. I won my share of tournaments after that, but had I kept a full schedule, I think I would have won more because I was playing pretty well then. Don't get me wrong, Ben's comeback was a great thing, and it showed just what kind of champion's heart he had and what kind of man he was. I'm just talking about that one year and the feeling of not being recognized by my peers.

It hurts even now.

## PLAYING FROM THE GROUND UP

I have always said, "Good players play from the legs up, and great players play from the feet up." Poor players, of course, hit at the ball—mainly with their shoulders, hands, and arms. I tried to look at the swing from the ground up, using the support of my legs to generate power.

I practiced barefoot a lot. I felt as if my feet were anchored into the ground. When you swing barefoot you feel as if your feet are roots digging into the ground and holding on or anchoring. At address, you feel your toes are almost up in the air and free. Your weight is established on the balls of your feet and somewhat back—never out on the toes. There is pressure down and on the inside of your feet, as opposed to outside, which is where most amateurs put it.

I always had good feel with my feet, too. But that was just a matter of experience. When I was a boy, once the spring fully set in, I didn't ever even think about putting shoes on until the first frost. One time, when I was a kid, I even caddied in the snow barefoot and got a serious frostbite.

You learned to be sensitive to your feet. In our backyard layout, you had to step carefully, if you know what I mean. You never knew what the horses and other animals might have left. I think it made me quick on my feet. I ran a hundred-yard dash in ten seconds in my bare feet once, and I always fancied myself a pretty fair dancer.

Footwork is more important than most golfers realize. It's the foundation for your balance.

# MASTERS MEMORIES

I have so many fond memories of the Masters and Augusta National Golf Club. I won the championship three times, in 1949, 1952, and 1954, and was the runner-up in 1939 and 1957. I look forward every spring to going to Augusta, to the Champions Dinner on Tuesday night and to starting the tournament as part of a group that includes Gene Sarazen and Byron Nelson.

So many memories are vivid in my mind, like playing two holes barefoot in 1942 after Fred Corcoran, my agent, had bragged about my ability to play barefoot. I birdied both!

In spite of eye trouble, I actually tied Rocco Mediate (among others) in 1990 for the Par Three championship held on the Wednesday before the tournament. Not bad—I was seventy-eight at the time!

My favorite memory is the famous 1954 Masters, which I won in an epic play-off with Ben

Hogan. My memory of that Monday play-off is so clear I could go out today and set the pins in exactly the same spots they were in that day.

Ben had won in 1953, but he wasn't hitting the ball very well that week in '54—well, not nearly up to the standards we had come to expect from him. He had made a lot of uncharacteristic mental and physical mistakes, even making a six at the par three twelfth hole in the final round.

# THE 1954 MASTERS

The 1954 Masters was second only to the 1942 PGA Championship on my list of favorite victories. The victory was extra sweet, not just because it was Augusta National, but because I beat Ben Hogan in a play-off. I always enjoyed going head-to-head with Hogan. I think any good competitor loves going against the best, and I felt my game rise up a notch against Hogan.

Let me set the stage for you. The '54 Masters is

famous not just for our Monday play-off but also for the fact that poor old Billy Joe Patton, an amateur, was leading the tournament on Sunday until he knocked the ball in the water on thirteen and then again on fifteen. Also figuring in here is the fact that I had won the Masters in '49, Hogan in '51, me in '52, and Hogan in '53.

I remember the play-off—every shot, every lie—as if it were yesterday. Before the play-off, which drew a huge gallery, I asked Ben if he wanted to split the purse, which was a thing we often did in play-off situations and I felt was fair enough. Ben took a couple of puffs on his cigarette and said, "Let's play," meaning that he had no intention of splitting the prize money.

Ben hadn't hit the ball particularly well that week. He could be awfully long off the tee, almost up with me, but this week he was hitting it short and crooked but keeping himself in competition with his great short game and putting. My putting was shaky all week, and it was beginning to fail me so much that this championship would be the last major I would win.

Hogan gave away less about himself than anyone I ever knew. He wished me luck on the first tee, and then he just froze. You always felt that there was nothing in the world important to him except his ball and how he would get it around the golf course.

We both shot thirty-five on the front side. And

just as they always say, "The tournament starts on the back nine." Only this time, it started on Monday, not Sunday. I made a three by holing a chip shot on ten and went up by one stroke, but Ben got it back when I plugged my ball in the back bunker on twelve, the short par three, and didn't get it up and down. I had to work hard just to make four—a bad shot could have gone into Rae's Creek and cost me the tournament. I hit a big tee shot around the corner on thirteen. Ben hit his shot to the right and walked all the way to my ball to examine my lie. I said, "Ben, I'm going for it," and after he laid up short, I hit a fairway wood in there, twenty-five feet from the pin.

On the fourteenth, Ben hit another poor drive, but he hit his second shot onto the green and two-putted from seventy feet. I hit a seven iron in and also made par. On the crucial par five fifteenth, I had to lay it up, but I made my five. Ben hit a three wood over the green. He had made a bad chip—in fact, several bad chips to this point—which was unlike Ben. He always seemed to take forever to hit his putts. On ten, I believe he smoked a whole cigarette before he putted!

On the sixteenth, which would turn out to be the decisive hole, the pin on that difficult par three was in the hardest position, at the back right of the green. We both played smart shots, leaving ourselves uphill putts. I putted first from about twenty feet and really slugged mine to get it up the hill. I thought I might have hit it too hard, but it came up a foot short. Then I thought to myself, "There's no way Ben will hit his hard enough to get up the hill." I even mentioned it to my caddie. Ben proceeded to hit one of the worst putts I ever saw him hit. From about fourteen feet out, he stabbed at it and left it five or six feet short. And then missed his second putt. As I was about to hit my second putt, someone yelled, "Miss it!" but it didn't bother me.

I still have nightmares about bad lies and things happening to me that I couldn't prevent. Well, it was almost a nightmare. Ben hit another weak drive, barely getting by the Eisenhower tree. The Eisenhower tree gets its name from the fact that my pal Ike used to hit his tee shot right into the tree on the left side of the fairway, leaving himself usually over two hundred yards to the hole. Ike said that they ought to take that tree down. Normally, of course, when the commander in chief makes such a remark, changes are made. But this is Augusta National, and the most powerful man around that place, club president Cliff Roberts, wouldn't hear of such a thing!

I hit a great tee shot, but I had an eerie feeling as I approached my ball. It was sitting on a dried-up divot, one of the *only* ones you'll ever see around a place as magnificently groomed as Augusta National. With no idea how the ball would fly, I hacked it out with a six iron instead of the eight iron I'd normally use from that distance. I gave a sigh of relief when I saw that shot land in the middle of the green. I made my par.

On the eighteenth, Ben hooked his drive into the second fairway bunker and I hit my drive up the right side—perfect . . . I thought. My ball came to rest about a foot from a sprinkler, and it had picked up a hunk of mud. I thought I might get some relief, so I called an official over. When I took my stance, some water seeped up from the sprinkler. The official said, "No relief, Sam, you can't 'make water.' " The lie was terrible, but he was right. It was just a rub of the green, a bad break. You can imagine the thoughts that went through my head, though.

Ben hit his shot to the front of the green, from where Houdini couldn't two-putt because the pin was way at the back. I hit my shot into a bunker and played it safe for a bogey, although my putt, which stopped on the lip, could have rolled all the way off the green had it lipped out. Ben *did* two-putt, proving he was a better putter than Houdini, but I had won, 70–71.

Bobby Jones said that this was the greatest golf match he had ever witnessed and the most exciting Masters of all time!

# LEFT HOLDING THE BAG

Back when I started playing, you couldn't use a private caddie to travel with you from tournament to tournament. You had to use a caddie who worked at the course where you were playing. That rule didn't change until not too many years ago. With that situation, you had to rely on the luck of the draw when it came to getting your caddie each week. Some of them didn't know one club from the other.

I had a caddie during the Masters named O'Brien who worked at the Augusta course. Well, we'd play our practice rounds and so forth and . . . well, let me tell you what I finally had to tell him.

I said, "O'Brien, if I get a little excited or something and ask you what club you think I should hit, you say, 'I don't know.' "

So I'm coming to the sixth hole, playing the par three, and I said, "O'Brien . . ." and I looked over at him and he shivered. He was afraid I was going to ask him to club me.

132

He said, "I ain't talkin'."

I said, "I'm not asking you what club I should hit, but do you remember which way the wind was blowing yesterday?"

He said, "You ain't going to give me hell." He didn't want to answer that question, either.

On the next hole we were all standing out there on the fairway, and the guy I was playing with asked his caddie what club he should hit. The caddie gave him the wrong club, and the player hit a poor shot with it. O'Brien turned to me and said, "Uh-huh, he don't know too much, either, do he?"

You can't put the blame on the caddie, though. It's like Trevino says when a caddie gives him, say, a seven iron, "He don't know how I'm going to hit that seven iron, whether I'm going to hit it full out, three quarters, or a knock-down shot," which is true.

Today, players have regular caddies who travel all over the world with them, and it works out well for a lot of them. The caddies get to know their players very well and can keep them relaxed and assured. It's got to help to have somebody there who's pulling for you day in and day out.

# TOUR SCHOOL—THE OLD DAYS

Today, people know the term "PGA School" or "Tour School" as the way the boys try to qualify for the PGA Tour. What *I'm* talking about are the clinics we held for the public before each tournament. They say we did a lot in my day to make golf more popular, and these clinics were one of the ways we did it. Boy, did people love to see us pros hit all kinds of different shots. These clinics were fun for us, too, but they could get a little embarrassing. One time, Bobby Locke got up there and the guy running the clinic wanted him to demonstrate how to hit a fade. Now, Bobby used to hook even his putts, so hitting a fade just wasn't something he could do easily. All of us pros knew it, but I guess that old MC didn't. Poor Bobby couldn't hit a left-to-right shot to save his life.

As part of these clinics, they used to have driving contests as well, and I used to win most of them. You'd win a little money for them, too. Not much. Just enough to go down there and have a couple of sodas.

I like to say that I swing with 85 percent of my power. I'd borrow from that leftover 15 percent during the driving contests. Don't get me wrong. I'm not saying I tried to kill the ball. In fact, when I wanted to hit it big, I'd bring the club back a little slower.

You see, the tendency when you want to hit the ball real hard is to jerk it back with your hands rather than keep everything together in one piece. What you want is the momentum going through the ball, not on your backswing. As Bobby Jones's teacher, Stewart Maiden, said, "You don't hit the ball with your backswing."

Anyhow, I would turn a little more, even though I had a big turn already. I'd also turn a little slower and gather my power up for that explosion at the moment of contact where it counts. In some of those contests it wasn't just how far you hit the ball, but it had to be in the fairway, too.

I'll never forget the time we were playing in Tennessee. At this one club, you'd come out of the pro shop, walk down the steps, and be on the first tee, where the driving contest was being held.

As I was teeing my ball up, I heard the screen door slam, bam! I looked around, and it was Hogan. He had his driver and a package of three balls, and

135

he stopped on the top of the steps. I went ahead and hit a good one. Well, Ben turned right around, went back in, put his driver away, and said, "I can't beat that."

## THE BEST PUTTER I
## EVER SAW

The best putter I ever saw was Bobby Locke, from South Africa. And not only was Locke the best putter I ever saw, but he could knock it in the trees, pitch it out, pitch it on, and make the putt for par. His pitch shots were soft lobs to the green—they had very little spin. Day in and day out he was the best ever. Locke had a closed putting stance and looked as if he batted the ball! But no matter what, if he was sixty feet away from the hole on the worst green you ever saw, he could knock it up within a foot of the hole.

Locke first came to the United States in 1946, I believe, and was tearing up the Tour. Some jealous players got the PGA to bar him from our events. I liked Locke a lot and wanted to play against the very best competition there was. I wanted to raise my game up, which I always seemed to do against Hogan and other really good players.

I helped to get Locke reinstated in the PGA so he could play in our tournaments. We played several exhibitions together. I went to South Africa—we traveled by ocean liner in those days—and played him and got thrashed! I got a good taste of how great pitching and putting could knock strokes off your score. I think I shot sixty-eight–sixty-seven in one thirty-six-hole match, and he beat me seven and six! In another exhibition, the greens were so bad they had cowlicks in them. A four-foot putt in a cowlick can make a complete circle! I missed eight putts inside a foot in one round. I lost a few matches to him because I had the worst case of the yips you ever saw! At first, everyone was saying that once I got my land legs I'd beat him, but I think I only won three matches. I could beat him thirteen–fourteen down in the thirty-six-hole matches from tee to green. But I was in such a bad state that Bobby wouldn't give me a four-inch putt!

Of the two phases of golf—you play one game in the air and the other on the ground—Bobby was the best at the ground game. He didn't look pretty putting—he moved his whole body—but he could putt any kind of green you had. If his ball didn't go in the hole, it was always close!

# Obstacles to Performance

In the early days of the Tour there were no gallery ropes and little in the way of gallery control. It could get noisy out there.

A few players might use some "gamesmanship"—making noise, moving while you were hitting, or saying something they thought might bother you. For the most part this didn't happen.

Noises, of course, can disrupt your concentration. I learned that the way I thought—or the way I talked to myself—disrupted my concentration in a more powerful way than any noises I ever heard on the golf course.

I did have a few tricks of dealing with galleries, though. One time one of my drives went into a man's coat pocket. I asked my caddie for my sharp wedge. The man turned white—he thought I was serious!

# U.S. OPENS LOST

People say I'm the best player to have never won a U.S. Open. It's not a title I enjoy having. To tell you the truth, until I got to be about forty-five years old, I *knew* I would win an Open. Sure, it bothered me a little that I had come close so often, but up until the time I knew my putting couldn't handle the slick greens the Open always has, I never thought it would happen to me.

People said I didn't have the nerves to win an Open, but I knew that wasn't true. I finished third in the 1974 PGA Championship at Tanglewood when I was sixty-two years old. I *knew* I could play championship golf. Lee Trevino won, Jack Nicklaus finished second, and I was just three strokes in back of Lee. Even then, though, it was my putting that failed me. I three-putted a few holes coming in, and there it went.

As best I can figure, after my first few Opens, it just worked on my mind a little. If I had shot sixty-nine in the final round of every Open I played in, I would have *nine* open titles. But it was my putting that failed me after the first few. The greens were always hard and slick, and I think I got too tentative, too defensive. I let tension creep in.

Writers said, "Snead's jinxed." Some were less kind and said I was yellow, that I lacked guts. I didn't see it that way. After years of trying to win an Open, I still had a positive attitude. I would tell myself that it took ten chances before I won the Masters, and then I won three in six years! I had endured my share of drubbings in the PGA Championship, not winning until 1942, and that after I was embarrassed by Paul Runyan eight and seven in the 1938 finals. I actually played better in that U.S. Open than in the others, but my turn hadn't come yet.

I played in my first U.S. Open at Oakland Hills in Birmingham, Michigan, in 1937. It didn't seem all that hard to me. I was in the clubhouse with a score of 283, which was one stroke higher than the all-time scoring record of 282 at the time. Everyone crowded around to congratulate me, including Tommy Armour, who said, "Laddie, you've won yourself a championship!" Armour was wrong. Ralph Guldahl was shooting up the place and came in with a 281 after a final round of sixty-nine. It was a disappointment, but it didn't eat at me the way others would.

My biggest disappointment came in 1939 at the

Spring Mill course at the Philadelphia Country Club. The final day featured thirty-six holes in those days, and I knew I was up to the challenge. I felt fit and ready. Coming to the seventeenth hole in the final round, I knew two pars would give me 281, and I was thinking back to how Guldahl had edged me out two years previously with a 281. On the seventeenth, I missed the green, chipped to five feet, and missed the short putt. That steamed me, and it was a bad time to lose control of myself because we didn't tee off for almost thirty minutes on eighteen, while marshals cleared the fairway. I thought I would need a birdie to win.

The final hole was normally an easy par five, and if I hit a good drive I could reach the green with my second. I think I really tried to lash into my drive, because I hit a diving hook.

My drive went about 275 yards and came to rest in a sandy lie. Still thinking I could make birdie if I knocked it on or near the green, I played a dumb shot. Using my favorite club, my old two and a half wood that had treated me so well, I topped the ball into a bunker. I chose an eight iron and gambled that I could hit the ball over the lip of the bunker and close enough to make my four. I "thinned" it, right into the face of the bunker. With an awkward stance, I had to make a baseball swing, and I hit the ball into another bunker. I was really hot now, but then the final blow came. Someone in the gallery told me that I needed to make a bogey to tie the leader in the clubhouse, Byron Nelson.

I just about snapped! If I had known that before I teed off, I wouldn't have been so darned aggressive. I pitched onto the green forty feet from the hole, charged my first putt, and missed my second coming back. A snowman, an eight! It was humiliating. All of my hopes and prayers were dashed, and I had made a fool of myself.

The very next year, at Canterbury in Cleveland, I vowed to do better, and I did, for a short time. I posted the lowest first-round score in Open history—a sixty-seven. I played poorly for the next three rounds and wound up nineteenth.

What happened in 1947 told me I needed a change. Lew Worsham went around the St. Louis Country Club in an Open record for three rounds—211—and posted a seventy-one in the final round. I needed a sixty-nine to tie. On the sixteenth hole, I missed a five-footer for a birdie and then a six-footer for a par at the seventeenth. My putting was a dismal sight!

I came to the seventy-second hole needing to make a twenty-foot downhiller for birdie. A thought popped into my head: Sam, you can do only one of two things—miss it or make it. Golf is a funny game some-times. I made that slippery putt as if I were Bobby Locke or Bob Jones! It gave me the confidence to think I could beat Worsham in the play-off on Sunday.

Lew battled me closely—sometimes too closely—in the play-off, but I never trailed him. I was ahead by one going to the seventeenth hole, where Lew made par. I missed the green and chipped to six feet. As I prepared to putt, Lew stood so close to me that I could hear him breathing. "Lew, step back and give me air." I was a little aggravated at his gamesmanship. I missed, and now we were tied.

On the eighteenth, I was right where I wanted to be, on the green twenty feet below the cup. Worsham was over the green but made a nice chip to what looked like a couple of feet away. I got too aggressive on my first putt and rolled it by. I lined it up and got ready to tap it in. The silence was deafening. The great crowd around the eighteenth green was deathly still. It was more like a murder trial than a sporting championship.

Just as I was about to take my putter back, Worsham burst the bubble of my concentration. "Sam, are you away?" Of course, I thought. But now a USGA referee was measuring to see who had the right to putt first. I *knew* I was away. I stood off to the side and stewed over this state of affairs as the referee determined to no one's surprise that I was thirty and a half inches from the cup—*and away.*

The delay seemed like a lifetime. The thoughts that came into my head were ugly. I wondered if I was going to be taken over by the demon yips. Would I be unable to take the blade back?

I hit a very weak putt that never had a chance. Worsham made his, and I was runner-up again! Bob Jones once said, "The Open isn't won, it's usually lost," and there I went again.

My plight and my putting wore heavily on me. I had my worst year in 1948 and decided I needed a change in my putting approach. I would do much better in 1949—Player of the Year, the Masters, Western Open, and PGA titles—$80,000 in winnings. Oh, and second place in the Open. Yes, golf is a funny game, and putting is the strangest thing about it.

## COPING WITH DEFEAT

I've won 185 professional golf tournaments. But I've "lost" around 400. Some of them I truly lost, and, in others, someone simply played better golf than me. I have mentioned many times how important it is to have a "will to win," but maybe just as important is how you handle defeat. In 1996, Tom Lehman won the British Open, the Tour Championship, and the Memorial. But he "lost" thirty events, including losing out to Steve Jones in the U.S. Open at Oakland Hills. How he handled the losses and the mistakes he made tells us more about the man than how he handled himself when things were going well. I'll always remember what Bobby Jones said on this point: He never learned a thing from winning but he learned a lot from his losses.

Let me say that it was my goal to win *every tournament* I entered, not to finish second or in the top ten. And I did my darnedest to win. You've got to have that fire to win. If I didn't win, well, I could accept that. I tried to figure out what I could do better next time.

The way I saw it, it was predestined anyway. I felt if it was my turn to win, I was going to win. I've come from behind a lot of times to win tournaments on the last few holes, but I've also had the other guy win, too. And that's life—those are the breaks. It was his turn to win. And breaks play such an important part in golf. One guy can have a beautiful lie in the rough, and I can have a bad lie in a divot in the middle of the fairway.

I did not like losing, not at all. I didn't like to lose at marbles, jacks, football, or golf, but losing is part of the game. When I lost a championship, I tried to find a way to think that would help me perform better. By believing that predestination played a big role I was able to cope with losing. I don't mean I

145

learned to like losing, I mean I handled it. I was driven to win. I don't think I ever gave up, but I could handle losing, too.

Maybe that's why sportswriters thought I had such a positive attitude. I gave the appearance of being happy-go-lucky, but nothing was further from the truth. I heard people say, "Snead doesn't try hard enough!" Lordy, I tried too hard, and all of the self-torture I put myself through at times didn't help. What did help was finding something good in the times when I got beaten.

Heaven knows, I tried too hard to win the U.S. Open. I finished second in my first one in 1937 and never won the thing, finishing second three other times. People said if Snead were like Hogan he'd have won five U.S. Opens. Maybe. Maybe not. Even up until I quit playing in the U.S. Open (when I was sixty-five years old at Southern Hills in 1977!), I felt that my failures in the Opens made golf fans more appreciative of me. Maybe they felt sorry for me or saw that I was human—capable of making mistakes—just like the ones they made when all they had to do to beat their buddy was two-putt from twenty feet. And then they three-putt.

I think if you're grim, solemn, and serious about golf—the way Hogan was, the way Nick Faldo is today—the writers and commentators never doubt your motivation to win or say you don't have the right stuff to win the big one. I think that's wrong, and I think it's unfair—you don't need to be grim to be motivated or serious. I admired Hogan, and I like the way Faldo plays. I admire the guy's commitment and his belief in himself. He's won six majors.

I wonder how losing the 1996 Masters will affect Greg Norman. I enjoy watching him play, and only time will tell if he can win the big ones. Gracious, he's had some awfully bad luck at times, and then at other times he's made some mistakes that cost him.

I heard Norman say that the 1996 Masters was a good learning experience for him, that he wouldn't fold up his tent and go home because he lost a seven-stroke lead. He said he got thousands of letters of support, so it seems as if he's got a good hold on his fans.

That reminds me of something Bob Jones said. He said the best stroke of luck he ever got in his storied golf career was that he didn't win the 1916 U.S. Amateur at Merion. At the time, Bob was a pudgy little boy—five feet four and maybe one hundred fifty pounds—and only fourteen years old. But he lacked the emotional maturity that he would learn rapidly over the next three or four years. Bob's temper got the best of him that week in spite of some often brilliant play. He led the field after the first round of qualifying but blew up in the second round. He won his first two matches, but he suffered bouts of temper, including hacking up a piece of the eighteenth green when he missed a putt, throwing his clubs, and hitting shots in anger.

Bob's good luck then was losing and having to confront criticism over his childish attitude, temper tantrums, and lack of composure. Of course, he was just a young buck and needed exactly what he got: some stern lectures from his father.

I hope Greg Norman has it in him to win several Masters championships. But I also wonder if the curse that visited me in the Open and Arnold Palmer in the PGA might keep him from wearing a green jacket.

## MORE ON PREDESTINATION

I know that many other players believed in predestination. Bob Jones was the most famous, I guess. He said that a golf tournament was all "in the book" before a shot was even hit. He tried as hard as anyone to win every event he played in (and he almost did!). If he didn't win he'd just say to himself, "I guess it wasn't my turn."

Bob had a great mental image that he once used. Back in Bob's day the marshals used megaphones to control the galleries. The megaphones would blast out, "Fore, please!" to warn the gallery to stand back while a player hit. On more than one occasion Jones would be barreling into the ball and a marshal would scream "Fore" into his megaphone, causing Jones to top his ball completely. Bob said that it made him think that, just like the angel Gabriel's trumpet telling us it's our time, the megaphone told him it *wasn't his time*—his turn to win.

I think it was this kind of attitude that made Bob Jones one of the greatest golfers of all time. He had a sense of peace, dignity, and grace about him that was almost eerie. He was one of the most self-composed men I've ever met.

Even when his formerly athletic body was ravaged by that awful degenerative disease of the spinal cord, syringomyelia, he was a model of strength, fortitude, and dignity. The last year he was at Augusta National was 1971, and I'm not sure if the story's true or not, but it's worth repeating. He was in his cabin, just to the left side of the tenth tee, when he was visited by one of his old friends, who was obviously upset by Jones's physical appearance. The man began to cry, and Jones said, "Now, now. We won't have that. We are supposed to play our ball as we find it."

# STAYING HOT WHILE
# KEEPING COOL

As I have said many times, a large part of this game of golf is about mastering yourself. Too many golfers get concerned about what others do and forget to do what they have to do to play the game.

You have to learn about yourself—what works for you and what doesn't. I think you need to be very competitive, very driven, but you need to be on an even keel on the course. Bobby Locke was as good at emotional control as anyone I ever saw. He didn't get too excited, and he didn't get down when he hit bad shots. He could wear you down if you let the ups and downs of a round get to you. And, man, was he a fighter. I liked that about him. You could shake your finger at him and he'd want to fight you, but that fire didn't show on every shot.

For me, the right intensity was "cool-mad." I discovered that if I got upset and angry on the course, I might as well pack it in because I wasn't about to play well. I found a way to stay intense but just a little bit above the action on the course—on that even keel. It helped me to focus on the next shot instead of spending all my energy trying to calm myself down. Cool-mad was what my high school coach Harold Bell called it, and it worked for me.

There have been many players in the history of the game who were great shot makers but were never consistent players or champions because they couldn't control their tempers. Tommy Bolt was one of the most athletically talented players of my era— he had every shot in the bag. But Tommy never realized much of his potential as a player, because if even the slightest thing went wrong—there went Tommy. Clubs would be flying around your head. Now, I am not saying that I haven't helicoptered a club or two—nearly all the great players have at one time or another. But not until they got control of their emotions did they really mature as players.

Bobby Jones was famous for "letting a club slip from his hands" when he was a boy, but, like all champions, he eventually won the battle with his emotions. I knew Bob (when he was an adult, of course) as one of the most dignified gentlemen I've ever met. Like any young person, he did things he later regretted, such as picking up his ball in anger over his poor play in the middle of a round at St. Andrews in the British Amateur championship. In one U.S. Amateur championship, he played against a fellow who was also throwing clubs, and people wondered how the winner would be determined if the other player ran out of clubs.

A similar story is told about Bolt, who was the world's greatest guy off the course but a raging bull on it. Tommy came to one par three of 135 yards and asked his caddie what club he should use. The caddie said, "Two iron."

Bolt said, "That's crazy, it's only a hundred and thirty-five yards!"

The caddie said, "But, Mr. Bolt, that's the only club we have left."

The point is that every golfer needs to learn how to control his emotions. Jones, Nelson, and even Nicklaus had their demons when they were younger. If you can't learn to conquer the demons, you will forever be an underachiever.

# GET A GRIP

I am quite sure that almost everyone comes up against the problem of losing control, and, in the course of their experiences, someone or something impresses upon you the need to be cool under pressure.

Jackie Burke, Jr., who won the Masters and PGA and is now at Champions Golf Club in Houston, got his lesson from his father, the famous teaching professional, Jack Burke, Sr. Jackie was eighteen and playing in a junior tournament in Houston, where he missed a short putt to lose a play-off. Jackie snapped and knocked his ball about a country mile off the green with his putter! Just then his father walked out of his gallery with flames coming out of his eyes and in front of the spectators read the riot act to his young son: "If you can't play without losing your head, son, give up the game!" Needless to say, it made a big impression on Jackie, and he went on to become a great champion.

Claude Harmon, Jr., now a fine teaching pro who has helped Greg Norman and Tiger Woods, among others, got treatment of a different sort from his dad, Claude Sr. Claude Jr., or "Butch," as he's called, had a problem with his temper when he was a teenager—and what teenager doesn't have a problem with self-control? Claude told me the quick cure for Butch's temper tantrums: He locked his son's clubs in the trunk of his car for about a month. From then on, Butch got a grip on himself.

# IF YOU CAN'T BREAK ONE HUNDRED, THE PROBLEM IS IN YOUR HEAD, NOT YOUR AIM

I have played in hundreds of pro-ams, and I make it a habit to watch how a player I might be able to help plays the game. I can usually tell if he has a chance to be a good player by the way he plays the game—

by his *management* more than his ball striking. As Ben Hogan said, "It's eighty percent management and twenty percent ball striking." I can teach a guy how to hit it better, but sometimes you can't help a guy who doesn't have the mental makeup.

Most amateurs try to hit the ball too hard—they go at everything 110 percent. I always tried to swing at about 85 percent power, even with my driver. When you go at it hard and try to hit it ten or fifteen yards farther than you should, your head comes off the ball and you get out of sync. You have to stay in sync, in rhythm. You can have a quick swing; some great players swing the club quickly, but it's *their own* tempo—it's their rhythm, and they can stay in sync.

There are two kinds of golfers—hitters and swingers. Swingers will last a long time because they keep in tempo, and, over the long haul, swingers will beat hitters. Hitters generate power with muscular effort—they try to create club-head speed with a hit. It's hard to stay in tempo when you hit *at* the ball.

Most amateurs are hitters, but I don't see too many hitters on the Tour today. Of course, when you try to get an amateur to swing within himself he thinks he'll sacrifice distance, so he doesn't want to make the change. Now, if you tell him he's aimed wrong or there's a driver that will get him more distance—he's all ears. He'll go right into the pro shop and lay down $500 for that driver.

When you give amateurs advice about their mental approach or management, only a special few players can make the adjustments. I might as well be telling my dog, Meister, about the stock market. But he'd rather be fishing.

## IMAGINATION

Byron Nelson liked to say that the best golf lessons he gave himself came at four o'clock in the morning. He would lie quietly in bed, in the dark, and picture in his mind his golf swing and the kind of shots he wanted to play that day. When he got to the course, Nelson found that those shots were easier to execute because he had been practicing them in his mind.

I always tried to picture each shot I hit before I hit it. Then it seemed as if I didn't have to think about it consciously when I got up to the ball.

I also used the time I spent traveling between stops on the Tour to think about the next tournament and the course we would be playing. I would "see" in my mind's eye how I could play each hole.

I think I did this naturally, as no one then ever talked to me about what they call mental practice these days. Being alone in the car on a long trip created the right mood—relaxed and carefree—to allow my imagination to work for me.

## PUTTING

Putting is so important in this game. If you can become a good putter and if you can drive the ball well, you can be a good player.

As I look back at my career, I think I was a good putter—especially a good lag or feel putter. I was never a great putter. But I don't think I could have won 185 tournaments around the world on all kinds of greens if I was not a decent putter.

The mistake I made was becoming a wrist putter. The only wrist putter I have ever seen hold up over the years is Billy Casper. If I had it to do over, I would have become an arm putter. I'd be a good putter today if they'd let me be an arm putter the way I want to be, using my old croquet style. I first saw a fellow using a croquet style in England. Right then I tried it, and I said to myself, "This is it. I can use my *arms* to putt, and I can see the line!"

I used the croquet style to win the PGA Seniors in 1965 and won it by fifteen strokes, and I made everything! I first used the croquet style on the regular Tour in 1966 at the PGA at Firestone. I started out the tournament putting the normal way, but when I double-hit a one-foot putt, I said, "That's it. I'm going to putt croquet-style." I had a five-footer for birdie on the very next hole, and I made it. But by 1968 the PGA had outlawed the croquet style and I had to invent my sidesaddle style.

Putting takes three things, in my opinion: confidence in your method, an ability to concentrate—both focusing on what you're doing and blocking out distractions—and the ability to relax under pressure.

For me, the lack of confidence in my stroke, some indecision, and negative thinking wrecked my putting. I had a good stroke that went bad when I got the yips, but, as I said, if I had started with an arm stroke—more the way I swing a club—it might have been different.

I learned a thing or two about the mental approach to putting, and I still think I could tell a fellow how to putt well. I learned from Bob Jones the importance of what he called "tranquilized breathing," or what we know now as deep breathing, to slow your heart rate down.

I probably worked too hard on the *mechanics* of my putting. Almost every night, I would take out a wooden yardstick and putt on the carpet of my hotel room, trying to keep my stroke square to the yardstick.

I was a very good greens reader. I usually could see the line of a putt pretty well. I had a good approach to putting strategy. For short putts, say, inside ten feet, I putted *at* the hole. I would aim the blade, for instance, at the left edge of the hole and stroke the putt solidly at the hole.

For longer putts, I putted *to* the hole. I tried to make the putt stop at the hole. I didn't want to have three- or four-footers coming back, so I emphasized the feel or weight of my putt so that it went the right distance. I don't go with some modern teaching that says putt hard enough to send the ball a foot and a half by the hole if it doesn't drop. The best putters I ever saw didn't do it that way. Jones saw three chances to make a long putt if the ball stopped around the cup: in the heart of the cup and falling in on either the left or the right side. If you putt more aggressively, you have only one chance—the heart of the cup. Major championship winners usually putt to the hole. I think of Nicklaus and Crenshaw today.

Their balls topple into the cup on longer putts. They putt *to* the hole, not *at* it.

Goodness knows, aggressive approach putts killed me! You don't need to be thinking about short comebackers. They weigh heavily on your mind. I think of the short putts I missed in the 1947 U.S. Open play-off with Lew Worsham as an example. You want to feel you can do it, see the line, get comfortable, and stroke it home.

# THE YIPS

If you use your small muscles and are a wrist putter, I think you are headed right for the yips. If you're constantly standing over short putts wondering if the devil will visit you—you've got 'em.

What are the yips, you ask? Bob Jones asked the same question of a legendary player once in England, who said, "Sonny, you'll know 'em when you get 'em!" It's true. In my opinion, the less said about this problem, the better!

# My Trademark Hat

I guess I take after my father in some respects. I always noticed how he hated people touching his head. Dad would want to fight anyone who kidded him about his balding head. He wore a big felt hat while he was working.

Just as I started making my way on the Tour, my hair started to fall out and I got pretty embarrassed about it. You can imagine the practical jokes played on me. I found a hat that finally felt right after trying plenty of different kinds. Playing golf can get pretty hot, so I needed something that would breathe and I found just the thing: a snap-brim palmetto hat. Back then, I was known as a sharp dresser, so I chose a hat with a fancy wide band. It became a trademark.

So even a negative like losing your hair can be turned into a positive. After all, not every golfer has a trademark!

# PRESIDENTIAL POWER

I have been fortunate to have played golf with some of America's great business, political, and sports leaders. I've played with kings and princes and just about every level of celebrity you can think of.

I played quite a bit with Presidents Eisenhower, Nixon, and Ford. I used to play with Ike and Nixon at the Greenbrier. One day we were on the thirteenth fairway and Nixon eyed a snake lying on a rock in a creek. I picked up a rock and threw it and killed the snake. When I saw Nixon in 1988 at the Waldorf-Astoria for the Centennial of American Golf, he walked up and said he'd never forget my killing that snake—from fifty paces away!

I could tell Mr. Nixon wasn't going to be much of a player when I first met him and played with him when he was vice president under Eisenhower. I think he wanted to be a better player—he was an ambitious kind of guy—but he wasn't much of an athlete. I tried to convince him that the short game—

particularly pitching and putting—was the way to lower his score. I knew he'd never become a good ball striker, but I also knew that he had great competitive instincts and that the appeal of cutting off strokes would be one he would like.

When I played against Bobby Locke in South Africa, I had gotten a good taste of how great pitching and putting could knock strokes off your score.

The effectiveness of my short-game argument was also seen in Mr. Eisenhower. Before I knew it, and much to the dismay of the press, Mr. Eisenhower had turned the White House lawn into his own personal short-game practice station!

I had a lot of fun with the presidents. I thought Eisenhower was the best player of the presidents I played with, although I'd say Dan Quayle was the best golfer of all the politicians I played with.

I gave Eisenhower quite a few lessons. We played at Burning Tree. He would wear those little glasses, and I discovered he wasn't turning very much because when he turned, he'd lose sight of the ball. I told him to turn a little more and that if he got new glasses with larger frames he could get a bigger turn and still see the ball. I told his doctor, who always played with us, to get him some new glasses and he said, "I'll do that. I'll do that."

But, you know, with Eisenhower everything was fast, fast. Couldn't slow him down.

I gave him a lesson one year at Augusta National that got his Secret Service people's attention. He was hitting it nowhere—again not turning his body. I said, "Mr. President, you've got to put your *ass* into it!" Well, I guess you weren't supposed to say things like that to the president, but it was true—you need to turn your hips and shoulders to get the power.

*Lee Trevino on Sam*

I think Sam Snead had the best golf swing of anyone I have ever had the pleasure of playing with. It was an absolutely flawless swing. Sam is a big man but very agile, and he swung with ease and grace.

I remember playing with him many years ago at the Diplomat. There was this tremendously long par four—we were both about 225 yards from the flag, and the wind was blowing hard against us. I couldn't reach the green, but Sam hit the most incredible shot. He took a driver and hit a high hook off the ground. I had never seen anyone do that.

Maybe the best way to teach the mechanics of the golf swing to a youngster today would be to have him or her watch videos of Sam Snead's swing.

You have to remember that Sam grew up and learned to swing a club without the benefit of a swing model like his. Golfers when Sam was a kid had little short, wristy, handsy swings. They were using wood-shafted clubs. They had weird-looking stances, and the clothes they wore! Those tweed coats looked as if they were five sizes too small!

Sam could hit all the shots, and you needed all of them on the courses they played in those days, which weren't in such great condition. Sam could hit the bump-and-run, the low shot, and the amazing thing was it looked as if he never had to change gears or change his swing to do it. I have watched Sam hit a lot of balls over the years. He's eighty-five now, and even though the RPMs have slowed up a bit, basically it's the same swing. It hasn't changed in all these years.

The Good Lord always gives people different talents to work with, but every once in a while a freak of nature happens. Sam is one of those. Jack Nicklaus is one, a man who has won eighteen major championships in golf, as are Jim Brown in football, Wayne Gretzky in hockey, and Michael Jordan in basketball. God has given them just that extra bit to be better than everyone else.

Sam gave me a lesson in 1968 at Rochester, just after I had blown tournaments in Houston and Atlanta. Roberto De Vicenzo beat me in Houston when I hit a three iron out on the driving range at the eighteenth hole at Champions. On the practice tee at Oak Hill I told Sam that I had a hard time getting the ball up in the air and no chance in a U.S. Open, where the greens are always hard and fast and I had no way of stopping my ball on those greens when they came in on such a low trajectory.

Sam told me I was moving too much on the ball, that I should try to stay behind it better. He said if I stayed behind the ball and let my hands release, the ball would have a better trajectory. I sure wasn't used to the feeling, but it was the best lesson I ever got. And, of course, I won the Open.

Older players learned the game by watching and copying—emulation. Most of them came from the caddie yard. Children are good at emulation. It's the best way to learn the golf swing. The average golfer could learn just from watching Sam's swing.

The secret to Sam's longevity is that he takes good care of himself. Sam is limber, strong, and supple even today. Also, I think Sam worked a lot harder than most people think. Sam wanted to win so bad. I think Sam sneaked off through the woods and hit a hell of a lot more practice shots than people thought.

---

# ON PRACTICE

I've mentioned that Ben Hogan liked to practice more than he liked to play and that Byron Nelson didn't seem to like to practice too much. Well, I loved to practice, and I still do. Here are a few tips to help you practice smarter.

- I think when you're hitting the ball well while you're practicing, you should quit. Don't hit too many balls, because eventually you'll fall right back into the problem you were trying to get out of. I've seen this happen to other guys, and I've done it myself: I'm hitting it so well in practice I don't want to quit! Even if you don't work yourself back into a bad habit, and your practice happens to be before your round, you might find that by the back nine you're tired and don't even know you are.
- Here's something I heard on TV. A guy said, "When you practice, you shouldn't shoot at a

target, you should work more on swing mechanics," or something like that. Well, what do you do when you get on a golf course? Don't you shoot at a target? All right, then. You need to get accustomed to shooting at a target in practice. What you want to do is work on what needs improvement. If you're fading it or hooking it a little bit, or if you're coming up short on your shots to the pin, or too long, that's what you want to work on. But don't work on it without a target!

• If you take some of those guys on the Tour today and put them out there on a flat piece of ground where they don't have anything to mark their distance by and tell them to hit a ball 125 yards on the carry, a lot of them can't do it. So many of them are so caught up in swing mechanics they don't work enough on their distance control. I'd work on 50-yard shots, 75-yard shots, 100-yard shots, up to 175-yard shots over and over. If you asked me to hit it fifty yards, I could put it within a couple of yards of fifty every time at the same time. I see players on the Tour today hitting it twenty, thirty feet from the pin with their nine irons! They're missing a whole lot of chances to make birdies because they're not practicing their yardage control enough. They have to hit the ball closer to the hole.

• The same is true with putting. When I'm playing with my son Jackie, I keep telling him that speed is more important than the line. Concentrate on the speed of the putt and it will save you a lot of three-putts. You develop that feel for the speed of your putts on the practice green.

I always like to practice with my shag balls—the tournament balls I'd toss in my shag bag after playing with them—and never those striped range balls. At the Greenbrier, I liked to practice by hitting over into the eighteenth fairway in the evenings when the course was empty. I liked those big trees out there so I could practice either cutting it around a tree, drawing it around that same tree, or hitting it right at the base of the tree. I liked having a structure to deal with just as you do on the golf course.

It's funny, because even though I liked to hook it and fade it, when it came to an actual shot on the course, I shot straight at the flag. You see, if you're a hooker and play it out to the right and that hook doesn't come off, you're in trouble. And if you're a slicer and start it out to the left and it doesn't slice back in, you're still in trouble. But if I aim straight at the flag and draw it or fade it a little I'm okay; I'm not too far from the hole. If the shot stays straight, well, I guess that's what they call a "good miss."

Motor learning, required for absorbing a skill like how to swing a golf club or shoot a free throw, comes in three stages.

Stage one is characterized by trying to get the fundamental picture of how the skills are performed. Typically, this stage is marked by gross errors, and efforts are aimed at reducing the severity of mistakes. Stage one is highly cognitive, meaning a lot of thinking happens. This is the stage where Sam practiced by himself, experimenting with a particular segment of his swing.

Stage two is where we begin to associate the skill with some previous success we have had with our kinesthetic (physical) or spatial awareness of the correct move.

Stage three involves little cognitive effort. Sam was the master of "no conscious effort." The skill simply runs off like a computer program—automatically—without our having to put a lot of attention into the movement.

When we are novices at a sport like golf, the brain has no model from which to work. Practicing lays down memories that allow us to make our skills durable and permanent. Later we are able to borrow parts of memorized programs the brain may have already stored. Sam used baseball, boxing, and other sports to associate his golf swing motions with, so he could steal from his memory bank.

Hard practice, therefore, is necessary to develop our skills to the point where they are grooved. Mastery is obtained only after the skill is overlearned. It is then that we can get into a high-performance mode where we simply trigger the start of the movement and the program runs on automatic pilot. We can then free up our brains to more important things, like competing, something Sam was a genius at.

---

# GREENSBORO: A FAVORITE STOP

I won the very first Greensboro Open in 1938, carrying away a winner's check of $1,000. For some reason I seemed to play well there. The courses we played, Starmount and Sedgefield, and the whole area and its people reminded me of home. I won eight Greensboro Opens. We would have a pre-tournament fishing tournament—which I also won on several occasions—and other activities that made the week fun.

They used to hold the tournaments the week before the Masters, so often the weather was cold. On one occasion I remember not being able to find a ball I had hit into a green because it was buried, not in the green but in the snow. So the tournament was not all roses. I got myself in trouble with the locals once—1960, I think—when I stated the obvious. The course wasn't in very good shape. I won the tournament, and I wish I had kept my bloody mouth shut!

# A WINNING "TREE" WOOD

They say golf is a "ball and stick" game, and I have a little story that proves it. I beat a guy at the Greenbrier by shooting a seventy-six with a wedge and a piece of swamp-maple sapling. In other words, with a wedge, a ball, and a stick.

I used to play this guy—Tommy Tomeo—using

my regular clubs. At first, I'd give him a stroke on all the holes except the par threes. Then I gave him a stroke a hole all the way around, then two shots on every hole that was over four hundred yards. Finally, I told him I would play him with a swamp-maple stick and a wedge.

Tommy said, "Let's see the stick."

A while earlier, I had pulled a sapling out of the ground and cut it down, so it looked something like a shinny stick. Then I took a hatchet and carved a little loft into the root area at the bottom to make a "club face" out of it. It measured about forty-five inches long, kind of the length of most of today's high-tech titanium-headed, graphite-shafted drivers. That stick was pretty heavy and stiff. It was actually thick at the bottom, then thinned down a bit as it moved to the top, just the opposite of a conventional golf club shaft, which accounted in part for its stiffness.

Tommy tried to hit a ball with it and couldn't get it off the ground, so he said, "I might have to give *you* strokes, Sam." I didn't say anything, but I thought, I don't think so.

I'd hit the ball pretty well with that thing, though. The seventeenth hole at Greenbrier is 525 yards, and I put it in the greenside bunker with that stick in two. I didn't use it on par threes because you had to swing it hard to get the ball in the air, which meant I couldn't hit partial or less than full-out shots with it.

As I said, it didn't have any flex to it whatsoever. I just killed poor Tommy with my wedge and stick.

Afterward, Tommy said, "From now on, hunting season's over!"

# GOLF WRITERS

I've been fortunate enough to have a pretty good relationship with golf writers through the years. I sure enjoy listening to a good yarn or even telling one now and again, and I guess they like to write them down on paper.

I was down at Augusta for the 1942 Masters when Fred Corcoran, a golf writer who was also my manager at that time, said, "Snead can play barefooted!"

A lot of the other writers said, "No way, you'd break your toes."

But Fred said, "No, he can play barefooted."

They didn't believe it. "I know he's your boy," they said, "but this is a lot of bull."

So Freddy came up to me and said, "I want you to play a couple of holes for me barefooted."

I said, "Freddy, you're at Augusta."

Gene Sarazen popped up and said, "Yeah, who do we have here, Huckleberry Finn?"

Well, Freddy put together a little bet during one of the practice days that I could play two holes barefooted. I birdied the first hole, then walked over and played the ninth, where I rimmed out for my birdie. That whole week, when those writers saw Freddy coming, they would turn around and go the other way.

Were things more relaxed then and more fun? I'd have to say, probably. Just look at the hordes of writers who swarm a player like Tiger Woods today—it's something else.

One time, Bill Smith of Charleston, West Virginia, wanted to interview me, but I was practicing, so I said, "Well, geez, I'm a little busy right now."

He walked away from me and muttered something under his breath like "you dumb" something or other.

I said, "What did you say?" So he repeated it.

So I said, "Well, come on, 'dummy,' come on, what do you want; what's bothering you?" and we did the interview. You know what? Bill and I went on to become the best of friends.

Down in Miami I was playing and Tommy Bolt

was already in the clubhouse thinking he might have won the tournament. Jimmy Burns was a golf writer for *The Miami Herald,* and he said, "That's nice going, Tommy."

Tommy said, "So you're going to talk to me now, now that I've won a tournament?"

Burns said, "Not yet, Tommy. Sam's still out there."

Well, I tied him on the last hole, then beat him in the play-off, so Burnsy and Tommy didn't have the conversation Tommy wanted that time. Jimmy Burns was another good friend. A writer at his paper used to say, "The trouble with Jimmy is that when he has nothing to write about, he always has a story to tell about Sam Snead!"

## BASEBALL AND ME

Baseball was one of my first loves and a sport I still enjoy today. I was a very good player, I think, and a good student of the game. I was a pitcher, a pretty good one, and I even toured around playing semipro ball. I applied my baseball experiences wherever I could to help me out of the fixes I got myself into in golf.

I played golf with many of the best baseball players in the history of the game. Some of them could really hold their own on the golf course. Ted Williams, Joe DiMaggio, Yogi Berra, and Mickey Mantle were among my favorites. The New York Yankees were the dominant team in my day, and I became close friends with many of the players. DiMaggio had the most talent for golf, but I don't think he played or practiced much. He carried a nine handicap and could shoot seventy-three in a pro-am. Jimmy Demaret and I told him he could be a scratch player if he wanted. He said, "No, I'll just take my nine." And then he won almost everything he played in.

Dan Topping was the owner of the New York Yankees for many years. He and I were close friends and played many rounds of golf together. We played some serious money matches at the Greenbrier over the years. I was with Dan when I caught the Atlantic World Record bonefish in Bimini.

Ted Williams and I were friends and spent many a day involved in our favorite other sport: fishing. He was a great fisherman and a great friend. If he hadn't served two tours in the service during World War II and Korea, he would have broken every record there was for hitting.

Williams did an analysis of my baseball swing for *Golf Digest* back in 1960. It was good fun. We always had a friendly rivalry going about something, whether it was hitting a baseball, hitting a golf ball, or fishing.

I analyzed his golf swing in the same article and said that Ted might have been the first southpaw golf champion. He had that delayed-hit action, holding his wrists back until the last second. But Ted was also a stubborn pull hitter in baseball (remember the famous "Williams Shift"?) and would have been a hooker in golf. He concentrated well, crowds didn't bother him, and he had a good touch, which I discovered watching him land large fish like tarpon on light lines. His vision would have made him an excellent greens reader. Yes, Ted Williams would have been an aggressive player on the Tour. I would have gotten a kick out of seeing Tommy "Thunder" Bolt and Williams playing together—both exposing their quick tempers!

Ted said I would have made a king-sized Yogi Berra if I played major-league baseball—a strong arm behind the plate to gun down stealing base runners, and that I'd hit the ball a mile.

We used to argue about which hand provided the power in the swing. I felt it was the left because you can pull more than you can push—you pull with the left hand in baseball or golf if you are right-handed. We argued about which sport was more difficult. The way Ted told it, baseball is harder because you have a man throwing a ball ninety miles an hour—and sometimes it's ducking away from you. You have about a tenth of a second to decide whether to swing. Maybe the pitcher doesn't like you and he throws one of those fastballs at your head! Williams always thought golfers were soft—nobody said "boo" on the golf course. The ball was just sitting there waiting for you to hit it. I'm sure he thought he was right.

I told him golf was harder because we've got to play all our foul balls. And you have no teammates to help you fit that little ball into a four-and-a-quarter-inch hole.

## HOLY COW, I NEED TO EXTEND MY ARMS!

Harry Caray, the famous baseball broadcaster with the St. Louis Cardinals, Chicago White Sox, and Chicago Cubs, has been one of my favorite announcers to listen to and to watch. I watched a lot of baseball, and I still watch quite a bit. In 1983, Harry inadvertently straightened out my swing with one of his comments on a broadcast.

Harry was telling about a hitter who got jammed and hit a weak ground ball to the infield. Harry said the reason was that the hitter didn't have a chance to extend his arms. I had been kicking around the house, a little concerned about a power leak in my swing. My ears pricked up as if I'd heard I'd won the lottery. I started thinking about it and made a few practice swings and discovered that Harry had given me just the tip I needed to correct my power leak. I needed to extend my arms through impact, not get all jammed and slide the club out there.

As soon as I got to the practice tee and found that extending my arms through impact was a good key, I started hitting it solid to center field. I heard Harry's voice in my head saying, "Cubs win! Cubs win!"

The day after practicing by extending my arms, I shot a sixty at the Lower Cascades. I was seventy-one years old. It just shows you that a good golf tip can come from anywhere. So keep your eyes and ears open, and be creative!

# TAKING WHAT THE LORD GIVES US

One of the biggest battles we face in golf when we get older is the battle with our nerves. Sure, we have our aches and pains. We lose some flexibility and some strength, but if we take care of ourselves it's not as bad as you think. Look at the fellows on the Senior Tour. They shoot some low scores!

I think when you've lost a little something you tend to react by tightening up. Your muscles aren't working as well, because they aren't as fluid. Your nerves want to make you force things to happen.

In 1983, when I was seventy-one, I shot a sixty at the Lower Cascades course at The Homestead, and I did it by just letting it happen, by resisting the temptation to force it. I was twelve under par going to seventeen, and I hit a three iron right at the flag. It looked as if it was going in the hole, but it went past by two feet. The green was not in good shape—it had a severe contour, and it's the worst green on the course—and I had to putt it up above the cup and try to make it come back down, but I missed.

On the last hole, I hit a four iron right at the flag again, and it looked as if it were going in for an eagle two. But it didn't, and I made a par for sixty. I think the Lord said, "Sam, I think you have had enough." Needless to say, I was very happy with my sixty.

# RYDER CUP CAPTAINCY: TEAM GOLF

By 1969, the Ryder Cup was gaining more publicity. Today's TV coverage and the addition of the top European players to the other side has had a lot to do with it. Now all the boys want to make the Ryder Cup team. I enjoyed being the Ryder Cup captain, but it wasn't always a walk in the park.

As captain, I tried to follow some of the old strategies about team competition. For instance, you don't pair together as a team a good putter with a bad putter, because if the good putter has a bad day, then you're in trouble.

Back when I was in the navy stationed in California, we had a team that played other military bases up and down the coast. I had two guys who couldn't break eighty, but, boy, I tell you, they sandwiched that ball together between them like you wouldn't believe.

Here's another. You don't team a big hitter with a short hitter, because if you're playing alternate shots, which is one of the Ryder Cup formats, the big hitter may say, "Gee, I've never been back here this far . . . I don't like this" when he has to play his partner's drive.

As Ryder Cup captain, you try to get two guys together who play the same, who hit it about the same length and have similar personalities. A guy might come up to me and say, "I can't play with him, I can't listen to his gab all the time; it upsets me. Give me somebody else, anybody!"

One time over there, I got all of the guys in one room before the match and asked them to put down on a piece of paper which two guys they'd like to be teamed with. When it was all over, we didn't exactly see it the same way. So I said, "Hey, I think I'm going to have to call back over to the United States and get another team sent over here." It was kind of tough.

Back to that '69 match, where Nicklaus conceded that last putt to Jacklin. That wasn't the only story involving Jack. He and Dan Sikes were going to be paired together in the morning match. The night before, I asked Jack if he'd rather rest and sit out that morning match so he could be really fresh for the afternoon singles match the same day. He said, "Okay."

I also wanted to give everybody on the team a chance to compete, and the opportunity of finding a match for them to play in was running out. I thought, Gee, if I were one of those fellas . . . well, one day down the road it might be . . . "Dad, did you ever get on the Ryder Cup team?"

And he'd say, "Yes."

Then it would be, "Who'd you beat?"

"Well, I never had a chance to play. . . ."

Along those lines, I thought it would be nice if everybody on the team could play.

Of course, the media got on this thing of me asking Jack to sit out, and maybe the whole story wasn't told, or even known to me at the time. I don't have to tell you that Jack was my best player, and, as I said, I wanted to keep him nice and fresh by not having him play two matches in one day. When you're playing every day, and sometimes twice a day, you get tired. Later on, Jack told somebody, "I wanted to play."

If he had said to me, "I'd rather play," he would have played. You know what the final word is on this subject? There was no animosity about it between Jack and me whatsoever.

## SCHOOL'S IN

I've had some good and bad things to say about teachers, but, if the truth be known, I actually enjoy teaching, particularly the Tour players. As I just mentioned, I did my best to help Tom Kite before the '97 Masters. Often the most medicine comes in the smallest pill. When I was watching him hit balls, I could see his right leg twitch at the finish of his swing. All I told him was that he was too tense over the ball.

I said, "Tom, just relax as much as you can. Let your arms hang down nice and straight and relaxed there at the ball."

He walked right up there, and, with the same

club, he hit the ball so much better, he thanked me three times. And he finished second in the Masters.

I was watching Tom Watson hit balls before he won the '96 Memorial. Now, Tom's still one of the best players from tee to green. His trouble is with his putting. Tom has told me that he used to watch me hit balls and tried to copy my rhythm and timing.

I appreciated the compliment, but, you know, Tom's tempo is quicker than mine, and it fits him just right as a person. You can't have a guy who's quick and a little jerky or whatnot and have him swing nice and slow and easy. That's not his forte. Such a person thinks quickly and does things quickly. Well, Tom Watson's rhythm looked just great to me for Tom Watson, and maybe he appreciated hearing me say so.

Sometimes a little praise is the best lesson anyone can give or get!

One of the best, or at least the funniest, lessons I gave was to Chi Chi Rodriguez in Honolulu.

Chi Chi said to me, "You know, Sam, I've been playing terrible the last part of the year. What's wrong with my swing?"

I said, "Swing? There's nothing wrong with your swing. Chi Chi, you know how you hit the ball and almost fall down?"

He said, "Yes."

I said, "You're falling down now before you

even hit the ball." All I did was get him to think a little more about balance.

He said, "If I win, you get five thousand."

He won only $350,000.

After the tournament, his caddie came into the men's locker room and had a check from Chi Chi for me. He said, "Don't cash it for a week."

## HAGEN DEFEATS HOGAN

Doug Sanders was one of the most colorful and talented players we had on the Tour in the fifties and sixties. Two things were distinctive about Sanders—the way he dressed and his short swing.

Doug was said to have over two hundred pairs of golf shoes—in every color of the rainbow—and matching shirts, sweaters, and slacks to boot. They called him the Peacock, he was so colorful. Sometimes you just shook your head when you saw him in his hot-pink shoes and outfit!

Doug's swing never got back far enough to get

off line. It wasn't a thing of beauty. It was fast, and if you blinked you missed it altogether. He could swing in a telephone booth. But the results were excellent. He won the Canadian Open as an amateur and won quite a few tournaments, but not as many as he should have.

Doug enjoyed life on the Tour. He probably had too much fun. One year he was on a roll—favored by the oddsmakers to win the U.S. Open at Canterbury in Cleveland. He got on his flight to Cleveland and met an attractive young woman who was going on to New York after a brief stopover in Cleveland. She invited Doug to go along with her and skip the U.S. Open. Doug said he heard the voice of Ben Hogan in one ear saying, "No, you've got to get to work. There are balls to hit! It's the U.S. Open." In his other ear, he heard the voice of fun-loving Walter Hagen saying, "There's plenty of golf tournaments to play. Stop and smell the flowers," or something to that effect. Needless to say, Doug skipped the U.S. Open that week, as Hagen won the match over Hogan for Doug's ear.

Up until a couple of years ago, Doug played very good golf despite a balky putter. He still lives in Houston and is as entertaining as ever.

Doug should have won the British Open in 1970. He had what would normally be a gimme putt on the seventy-second hole but had an unfortunate attack of the yips. Nicklaus beat him in a play-off the next day. Many people still ask him if he thinks about that little putt and the missed opportunity. Doug says he hardly ever thinks about it—only once a day over the past quarter of a century!

## STAR SEARCH: PLAYING WITH CELEBRITIES

I loved playing with Bob Hope and Bing Crosby. I won their tournaments on several occasions, and we played lots of social and exhibition golf together. They got as much mileage out of me as I did them. We were always giving each other the needle. Crosby, who was a pretty fair player and played in the U.S. Amateur a few times, told this story. He told me he'd won the Academy Award, and I was supposed to have said, "Great! Was that match play or medal play?"

Bob Hope had a lot of fun with me, too, as the target of his jokes. He told one about my being asked if I'd played in Iraq, and I'm supposed to have said, "No, who's the pro there?"

Years back I put together a little tournament out in L.A., where I'd play matches with different celebrities. I'd play with people like Jim Garner, Randolph Scott, Jerry Lewis, Mickey Rooney, and Robert Wagner. In fact, Bobby Wagner was the only one who beat me in the whole thing, and he didn't really beat me. I had a four-footer to tie him, and I just raked it away to give him the match. Since we were using the handicap system, they all got strokes.

Well, Bobby, who later starred in *It Takes a Thief* on TV, jumped four feet straight up in the air and screamed, "I beat this son of a bitch!"

We gave away golf bags as prizes, and he said, "I don't want any golf bag, I want a six-foot trophy!"

I said, "Come on, Bobby, you wanted me to make a four-inch putt?" I guess I shortened it just to rib him a little. A few years back I saw him and decided to put the needle in a little further after all this time. "Bobby," I asked him, "are you still a thief?"

Another time I was playing with Harpo Marx, who had his wig and the whole getup on. Well, he hit his ball up near the green, and it wasn't sitting in too good a lie. He wanted to roll it over with his foot to improve the lie, but I said, "No, no, you have to play that ball as it is."

Next, he started doing that whistling thing he did and everything that went with it, so I figured I'd help him out. I walked over and took another look at the

190

ball and said out loud for everyone to hear, "Ground under repair!" meaning he was entitled to improve his lie. Then I said, "Okay, you have to drop the ball properly over your shoulder."

So he turned around with his back to the flag and threw the ball over his shoulder right onto the green! I guess Harpo was pretty good at bending the rules.

Jerry Lewis was also a lot of fun. I got to the practice range one day and Jerry was telling everybody that he had a one iron that was the best one iron made. I told Jerry to try mine, and he said, "Let me hit it."

He hit the ball far better with my club than with his, so he said, "I've got to have it, I'll give you a hundred for it."

I said, "No, no."

He said, "I'll give two hundred."

I said, "No, losing that club would ruin my whole bag."

He said, "I'll give you five hundred."

I said, "Run with it before I change my mind."

I understand Jerry has that one iron displayed nicely in his den now.

A lot of today's celebrities love their golf, but I don't think anyone enjoyed the game more than Jackie Gleason. He was a pretty fair player, too. Jackie played a little billiards in his day, and what is that but another game where you put a ball into a hole with a stick?

Anyway, Jackie and I were partners in a little celebrity exhibition against my fellow Tour pro Art Wall and his celebrity partner, bandleader Fred Waring. I looked in Fred's bag on the first hole and he had all wooden clubs, no irons, except what he called his "trouble club," which looked to me like a slightly oversized four iron. He'd use that thing if he were in the rocks or some other rough place and he didn't want to scar up his wooden clubs.

The thing is Fred had a pretty high handicap, so when he went out there and made natural pars on the first three holes, I turned to Jackie and said, "Good Lord, have mercy!"

Jackie said, "Don't worry about a thing, son. All the four wheels will run off, even the spare." He was right, and Fred came back down to earth and the pars started to dwindle.

Now, on one hole, Art and Jackie were in a greenside trap. Jackie had a good lie, but Art's ball was buried in the sand. It was an impossible situation even for a fine trap player like Art Wall. So Art tried to blast out and left the ball in the sand. Then Jackie went ahead and holed his shot from the trap! He was so excited, he forgot his golf cart and ran on up to the next tee. After his drive, Jackie turned to me and said, "Lord, I'm so shook up, I lost my horse . . . I better go back and get it."

The result was that we won the match and were ready to celebrate. Jackie liked champagne, and at the party that night, he drank two bottles of the bubbly, then wandered out on the golf course and passed out. Well, it took six men and a pickup truck to bring him in!

To the victors go the spoils . . . and sometimes the headaches.

# The Day the Senior PGA Tour Was Born

Jimmy Demaret was one of the great personalities in golf. He won his share of championships and became a friend to just about everyone in the game. Later in his career, Jimmy became the host of *Shell's Wonderful World of Golf* and traveled all over the world as a golf ambassador. The producer of *Shell's Wonderful World of Golf* was another clever man, Fred Raphael, who practically invented televised golf.

Jimmy and Fred were bemoaning the fact that as the late 1970s came along many of the most colorful players had long passed their prime. Gene Sarazen was in his seventies, I was in my sixties along with Demaret, and there were some youngsters like Gardner Dickinson, Peter Thomson, and Roberto De Vicenzo who were over fifty. Right around the corner were the likes of Arnold Palmer and Gary Player, and, ten years down the road, Jack Nicklaus, who would soon be too old to compete with the flat-bellied college boys.

Demaret and Raphael cooked up an idea that no one knew would be so wildly successful. They proposed a tournament, the Legends of Golf, that would allow seniors to pair up in teams and compete against other senior players. We played the first one in 1978 at the Onion Creek Country Club in Austin, Texas, and television took a chance on the potential market for this kind of game.

I played with longtime buddy Gardner Dickinson in that event and, sure enough, the adrenaline and magic were there at the end, much to the delight of the television audience. I birdied the last three holes of regulation to beat Peter Thomson and Kel Nagle by one stroke. That started it all, and now the Senior Tour is healthier than ever.

# GOLF COURSE DESIGN

While I was in the navy in San Diego in 1943 and '44, I designed golf courses for servicemen stationed at the naval bases. I designed three or four in the forties, and then, in the late fifties and early sixties, I began giving golf course architecture some real thought. I was good friends with Donald Ross and later a business partner of Robert Trent Jones, both top-notch designers.

I knew what I liked in a golf course, and I had some good tutoring from Ross and Jones. In the late 1980s, I took further steps to design courses, and I have done seven in Japan, courses in West Virginia, Savannah (with Bob Cupp), and at the World Golf Hall of Fame (with Gene Sarazen and Bobby Weed).

The courses I admired the most, particularly the Upper Cascades near Hot Springs, the Old White Course at the Greenbrier, and old Pinehurst Number Two, had certain classic characteristics that made them enjoyable and challenging to play. I feel that a golfer likes to see where he wants to hit the ball, with no abrupt changes in the terrain to upset his eye. A golfer likes to look down from the tee with room to bail out.

I like greens to have several good pin placements and have at least seven thousand square feet, with no elephants buried in them! I don't like the idea of triple-tiered greens, but I do like greens to have slope so that you can read them. Greens that are flat as your dining room table are hard to read. I don't like greens that slope away from you in the back or greens that pitch hard toward the water. I think chipping and decision making on different shots around the greens have been taken away in modern golf course architecture, so I've designed plenty of chipping areas.

Par fives shouldn't have bunkers in front of the greens, and long par fours have no business having those huge, cavernous bunkers in the fairway. Par threes shouldn't play more than 185 yards from the regular tees for the typical club golfer. I especially like to have one short par four that's drivable for a longer hitter but will give him trouble if he's crooked off the tee.

Golf courses should be challenging but also fair and honest. They should also take better care of the guys who pay the freight. Some municipal and resort courses are so hard and long that an average player has a hard time having fun. It's no fun to lose half a dozen balls, either—in the woods or the water.

Golf courses should fit well with the land, be pleasing to the eye, and be places you can have fun. I think of planning a course around a property, not forcing it. It's like painting with a broad brush, with no sharp angles or tall mounds. I want the course to flow and roll with the land as much as possible.

# PRO-AMS

Today, a tournament's pro-am is a big deal, with many of the executives from an event's corporate sponsors enjoying their day out with the pros. The guys on the Tour need to treat these businessmen well because they're the ones whose companies are paying the bills. The amateurs in pro-ams today are generally pretty experienced, even serious, about golf, and it's a standard punch line out there for one of the boys on the Tour to say to his amateur partner after he hit a good shot, "You're spending too much time on the golf course, and not enough time in the office!"

Back a way, pro-ams were important, too, but

maybe they didn't have all the hoopla attached to them the way they do today. We saw playing in those pretournament rounds with our amateur partners as another way we could spread the word about what a great game golf was here in America. Maybe this is my way of saying that some of those guys weren't as experienced as they should have been to be out there playing in front of fans who had come out to see us pros.

I like people and have met a lot of nice folks playing in pro-ams, but I have to say my mind was already on the tournament coming up and I used the pro-am rounds to get more familiar with the course and to practice for the main event.

But I'll tell you what, golf is golf, and as you're the pro member of your team, you kind of get drawn into the pro-am action. I even used to have my own tournament called "The Sam Snead Festival," which wasn't a pretournament pro-am, but it certainly resembled one.

On one round, one of my partners wasn't doing very well, so I told his caddie to give him two more clubs than he wanted on every shot. The guy thought he was twenty-one years old, I guess, when he was about seventy.

The caddie said, "No, no, I couldn't do that." After all, the player was boss for the day.

So I said, "Do you want to win this tournament?"
The caddie said, "Hell, yes!"

I said, "Just listen to me and give this guy the club I tell you to."

Next hole, my partner hit his drive, and I asked him what he was going to hit to the green. He said, "Seven iron."

I said, "You can't get there with a seven iron. Take the four iron."

He took the four iron, put it ten feet from the cup, holed the putt, and got a shot-a-hole handicap. That's a three for a two, or a natural birdie for a net eagle. If he hit that seven iron, he's looking at a bogey even with the stroke he got on the hole.

It kept going this way until we got to the fifteenth hole, where he wanted to hit a five iron to the green. I said again, "You can't get there with a five iron. Take the two iron."

He knocked the ball a little over the green, then turned to me and said, "You see, I hit it too far with that club."

I told him, "If you'd got it up in the air a little bit, it wouldn't have run like that, and might have gone in the hole."

The pro-am got a big boost with Bing Crosby's tournament. As everybody knows, Bing created an event that paired Tour pros with his amateur friends, most of them entertainers and celebrities like himself. They called it a "clambake," and, boy oh boy, Bing put on one heck of a party.

I won the individual pro part of the first two Crosby tournaments, in 1937 and 1938, which were played in San Diego. Now, in one of them I had this guy as my amateur partner who never helped me on a single hole. We won the thing, and the guy got a trophy that looked as if it were five feet tall. You know, that S.O.B. never even paid my caddie!

These amateurs love to win, but let me tell you something: for the most part, they're as nervous as all get-out. You can just see them shaking.

After the Crosby moved up to Pebble Beach, I had an amateur partner named Roger Kelly one year. He was a lawyer with a six handicap out there in California, so the guy could play just a little bit. When he got up there at the start of the tournament, he vomited right on the first tee box. Roger calmed down pretty quick, though. As I said, he got six strokes, and, you know, he almost birdied every hole he received a stroke on. We won the thing going away.

The other guys were hollering and hollering about it, thinking he was some kind of sandbagger. So I said, "Wait a minute, he had the ball in his pocket half the round, out of the holes completely. Heck, I finished second in the tournament among the pros, so what are you hollering about?"

A guy makes a couple of birdies and everybody's screaming!

# WHY WE CAN'T PLAY THE WAY WE HIT IT ON THE PRACTICE TEE

Most golfers, even average golfers who play a couple of times a month, have the experience of hitting the ball very solidly and accurately a lot of the time on the practice ground. Similarly, even the amateur players I play with today can make serviceable-to-good practice swings. The fundamentals are there, and when the players go at it for real, everything seems to fall apart. Why?

Most amateurs I see go at the ball too hard. Their practice swings are nice and smooth. If they tried to swing at 85 percent instead of 120 percent, I think they could maintain the fundamentals of a good swing better.

The other thing I feel is that golfers get too caught up in the results—in what the ball should or should not do. I know this happened to me, and when it did I simply reminded myself that my *performance* was what counted, not necessarily the *result*. By this I mean that I focused on my good practice swing and not on the bunkers, lakes, or out-of-bounds stakes. You have to almost trick yourself, saying you don't care where the ball goes, that you only want to make the swing you know you are capable of making.

I'm not saying it's easy to do. It takes courage and mental toughness to count on yourself to make your normal swing when the pressure's on, but I know it's the best way not to allow the demons to take over and jump at the ball.

# BEYOND GOLF

My wife, Audrey, passed away in 1990. She was the best friend I ever had.

My son Jackie lives with his lovely wife, Ann, in a house just a five iron downhill from me on the Olde Snead Links Farm in Hot Springs. They run our golf-related businesses and do a fine job. They also watch out for Terry, my younger son, who is still a joy in spite of his struggles.

I have always had plenty of other interests and hobbies. Hunting and fishing were passions for me once, but today I can't see killing animals, so I don't hunt anymore. I love to fish, and I still take my dog, Meister, three or four times a week. I was mighty proud that I held a world record for bonefish for many years. Fishing puts me back in touch with the peacefulness of natural things.

When I can't play golf or fish, I like to play cards, particularly gin rummy.

# MY BEEF WITH THE PGA

When I looked over my own records and the scrapbooks that the Greenbrier kept on my career, I discovered that I won 185 professional golf tournaments. Some of those were unofficial events, not sponsored or run by the PGA but by other state PGAs or by a club. The money I won spent just as well as my official PGA Tour money winnings of $620,126.

The PGA Tour credits me with eighty-one "official" tournament victories. Jack Nicklaus has won seventy-one official PGA tournaments. At one time, the PGA had me down for eighty-four Tour wins. I have been worried about the fact that Jack may not win another tournament, but if they keep taking tournaments away from me, Jack may overtake me on the all-time tournament victory list.

It really eats at me, and with the help of my friend, attorney, and golf partner, Jack Vardaman, I've asked the PGA Tour to take another look at what happened. Here's the way I see it.

During the years I played the Tour from 1936 on, it was run by the PGA of America, the predecessor to the current PGA Tour. The PGA of America conducted the tournaments, established the rules and regulations, and maintained statistics about the Tour and its players. Each year it published a Tour media guide that included profiles and a list of Tour victories. My last victory on the regular PGA Tour was in 1965, and up through 1985 I was always credited with eighty-four Tour victories. The 1986 *Official Media Guide* has me down for eighty-four. Other historical volumes, such as the *Guinness Book of Golf Facts and Feats* and the 1988 *Encyclopedia of World Golf,* claim I won eighty-four.

In 1986, the PGA Tour, which took over the running of the Tour in 1968, started a project that included writing a history of the Tour and keeping its official statistics. Part of the job was to determine which tournaments were official and which were unofficial. The PGA of America didn't really have a strict definition of the differences between official and unofficial. As a matter of fact, certain tournaments were counted for the Vardon Trophy (the award for lowest stroke average on tour), certain ones counted toward qualifying for the Tournament of Champions, and still others counted toward official money winnings. And still others counted for Tour victories for the media guide. Confused? Well, so am I!

The PGA Tour tried to resolve which tournaments were official and which were unofficial by appointing a special committee charged with the responsibility of determining which unofficial events should be regarded as officially of historical significance. Players were then given credit for tournaments that were official or of historical significance. This committee determined that six tournaments, not included in the eighty-four that I *had* credit for, should be added to my victory list. These tournament victories were:

> 1937    Bing Crosby Tournament
> 1938    Bing Crosby Tournament
> 1941    Bing Crosby Pro-Am

1950   Bing Crosby Pro-Am
1952   Palm Beach Round Robin
1957   Palm Beach Round Robin

Then, at the same time the committee added six tournament victories, it took away eight I had always been given credit for by both the PGA of America and the PGA Tour. They were:

1939   Ontario Open
1942   Cordoba Open
1952   Greenbrier Invitational
1952   Julius Boros Open
1953   Greenbrier Invitational
1958   Greenbrier Invitational
1959   Sam Snead Festival
1961   Sam Snead Festival

Currently, the PGA Tour and its *History of the PGA Tour* give me credit for only eighty-one tournament victories. I may not have been that great in mathematics in school, but even I don't think that $84+6-8=81$! More important, I don't think their logic is right.

It seems to me that if the governing body of professional golf in the United States during the time I played was the PGA of America, then this group should get to decide what's a Tour victory and what's not. It gripes me that you can have a new governing body take over and change the rules and therefore the records. If the PGA of America said at the time that it was a Tour victory, then it's a Tour victory and it is of historical significance.

I can't imagine that Bud Selig, acting commissioner of major-league baseball or whatever they call him these days, will take away several of Babe Ruth's home runs from 1927 because the right-field fence in Yankee Stadium was shorter than it is today or because the ball was too lively then. It just isn't done.

What if you took away credit for winning a heavyweight championship bout because it was held in Zaire or Manila? Of course, it isn't done. But it was done to me. For example, I think I lost credit for the Ontario Open in 1939 because it wasn't held in the U.S. Yet look at examples of other players who have kept their victories for events outside the U.S. The ones that come to mind are:

| | | |
|---|---|---|
| Gene Sarazen | 1928 | Nassau Bahamas Open |
| Byron Nelson | 1945 | Montreal Open |
| Ben Hogan | 1946 | Winnipeg Open |
| Dutch Harrison | 1958 | Tijuana Open |

I feel that I won a number of other tournaments that included the top players of our time and still did not get credit for an official victory.

I am flattered, though, that in its analysis of records the PGA Tour listed me as the number one player of all time, reflecting the fact that I competed against many of the best players the game has known and came out on top more often than anyone else.

---

## Dan Quayle on Sam

---

I have had the honor and privilege of knowing Sam Snead for many years and have enjoyed playing with him on many occasions. I was fortunate enough to host an eightieth birthday celebration in honor of Sam, Byron Nelson, and Ben Hogan. It was a special event, and the participants went away with a feeling that they had been in the presence of greatness. I know I did.

My wife, Marilyn, and I were responsible for the seating arrangements for the dinner we hosted at the vice president's residence at the Naval Observatory. Having been in Sam's company at many a dinner, I knew our guests were in for a treat. Sam would probably tell many of his old stories and some new ones—Sam was renowned for his stories. The more I thought about this prospect, the more I worried about the seating arrangements! Marilyn and I had placed Sam between her and Supreme Court justice Sandra Day O'Connor. Before we sat down to dinner I made Sam promise to behave himself.

Sam often tells a story about a round of golf we played at The Homestead that attracted some attention.

Sam said, "I wasn't playing too good, and Dan was playin' great. By some *miracle* he beat me out of ten bucks. I gave Quayle a twenty-dollar bill and he went into the pro shop to get change. When he came out, a crowd of people had gathered. They saw the vice-president give me a ten, and someone said, 'Sam, looks like you beat the vice president.' I smiled and said, 'What does it look like?' "

I guess this proves the old political adage that appearances are sometimes more important than reality.

Sam always made it a point to have fun with every round I played—win or lose. I know my limits. I had faced off in negotiations and debated with Boris Yeltsin, Margaret Thatcher, Al Gore, and others whom I felt I could beat. But with Sam Snead, even if you manage to beat him, he always comes out on top. I had met my match.

# MY EIGHTIETH BIRTHDAY

When he was vice president of the United States, Dan Quayle organized an eightieth birthday party celebration at the vice president's house on the grounds of the Naval Observatory in Washington. The party celebrated the birthdays of Hogan, Nelson, and myself. It was quite an affair and such a great honor. But poor Ben, whose health had failed him in recent years, couldn't attend.

Gene Sarazen, who was ninety that year, was also present. He told President Bush that he had visited the Oval Office once before, seventy years earlier, in 1922, when Warren Harding was president. Gene had been invited by Harding after winning the U.S. Open at the age of twenty.

Before lunch, we visited President Bush in the Oval Office. He asked me to give him a lesson right out on the lawn. He said he was having trouble and was shanking his pitch shots. Sure enough, he shanked two or three balls when he showed me. I showed him a technique that was a little bit better, and now I am wondering, since he's left the White House and has had more time to practice and play, if he's cured those shanks.

George Bush is a great leader and a great man but a bad chipper and pitcher. If you read this book, Mr. President, come on down to Hot Springs and I'll get your game on the right track!

---

## Fran Pirozzolo on Feel

---

We are constantly admonished to feel the shot we are trying to hit, as much as any instructional piece of wisdom. For an unfortunate few, we might as well be told to feel like a billionaire, because that advice just doesn't give us the necessary resources to perform the job. Even among skilled professionals, the feel of a swing deserts them at times.

What is feel, anyway? Can it be developed to a higher level in average players? And how would we practice feeling a shot, as Sam did, so that the memory trace of our swings is more durable and resistant to decaying over periods when we can't practice like the pros?

The feel of a golf swing is the kinesthetic awareness (of body sensation) of the sequential motions—both in space and time—of the swing. It is the brain's internal representation of your stroke, the memory of how your body moves through space and time to hit the golf ball. Because we have a blueprint for how we swing the golf club and have rehearsed it to a certain extent (or practiced it, if you prefer), we can direct our brains to a location that has stored this particular memory. I confess that this sounds complicated precisely because we must use words to attempt to describe a sensory perception. But don't get discouraged—it would be just as difficult to define or describe the smell of an orange or the sound of a railroad engine steaming toward you. Fortunately, we all can recognize the smell of an orange. So, too, should we be able to recognize our golf swings.

Can feel be developed? Of course it can. Most of us can ride a bike. We learn (through practice) the sequential motions, timing, and balance to enable us to ride a bike without falling.

We all differ in our God-given abilities to perform the motions necessary to execute such a precise movement as the golf stroke, but the sad fact is most of us could improve our skills much more than we think. I believe that the ceiling may be set for our kinesthetic gifts at birth but that most of us helplessly accept results closer to the floor than we should tolerate. We definitely can improve our feel, just as we can cultivate our skills in cognitive, emotional, and other physical domains. We should be trying to blueprint a feel of our best swings, trying to re-create the memory of a good swing. It's best to try to clear your mind before you practice. Try to blend your movements to a sound or rhythm, much as Bobby Jones and Sam Snead did. They heard a rhythm in their minds, giving their swings the same rhythm as the melody they "auditorized." By associating your swing with sound, and *certainly* through visualization of the proper moves of our swings, we can make the memory or feel of our swings easier to call up.

Remember that practice makes perfect, so find the right moves and practice hearing, seeing, and feeling the best swings you know how to make. Drills are good to perform in combination with your full swing practice, because they may more clearly isolate a part of your swing (such as the takeaway) that is less than perfect. By giving it an emphasis through drills that heighten the ideal feel of that segment of your swing, you will be blueprinting the correct movements that have eluded you previously.

The more childlike you can make your practice, i.e., the simpler and more fun you can make it, the better you will learn. In general, children have a more untroubled contact with the realities of learning more skills, and this attitude sets the stage for rapid learning.

# WHEN SOMETHING'S NOT RIGHT ABOUT YOUR SWING

I believed in my swing and in my system of playing the game. When things went wrong for some of the boys, they'd doubt themselves and want to develop a whole new swing.

I always told myself, "When things go wrong, try not to change a thing." My keys were tempo and timing. Also, you want to return the shaft to the same angle it started. If you can do that, you will start hitting the ball straight again.

I would go to the range and hit a bag of balls with a mid-iron, just trying to return the shaft to the same angle where it started. Usually when you get off, the shaft comes in higher than it started and you hit over the top, as we say. From there, it can go right or left.

I would try to take the club back slowly with everything moving together. One of the main things I see with amateurs is that they allow tension to build up and they "snatch" it back. I used to tell my amateur friends that if they "snatched" a fork the way they "snatched" the club back, they'd starve to death.

## QUAYLE HUNTING

Speaking of former vice president Dan Quayle, heaven knows he had his share of troubles in office. It's funny how different a man can be from the way the media views him. In the middle of his term as vice president, we were scheduled to play a round together. I knew he was a little stressed out at work, and I was looking forward to being able to have a fun, competitive round. Of course, I knew we would have ten or twelve Secret Service men spread out all over the course, and they would be a bit of a distraction.

I had gotten a brand-new red sweater that I thought was pretty neat and decided to wear it for our round. Sure enough, Mr. Quayle showed up with a red sweater on. Now I was worried. What if some nut showed up and started shooting—he might mistake the old guy in the red sweater for the vice president!

# THE BIG THREE

I don't understand it exactly, but it sure does seem that the Lord gives us what we need at decisive points in history—as if, as I have said, it's all pre-destined. Golf in America got a shot in the arm when a caddie-turned-player, Francis Ouimet, bested the big boys from Britain, Ted Ray and Harry Vardon, in the 1913 U.S. Open. Bob Jones created an interest in golf through his incredible accomplishments as an amateur golfer.

Some say Sam Snead and his pals barnstormed around the country and introduced more and more people to the game and to the Tour. Ben Hogan, Byron Nelson, and I did a lot to make golf more popular in America, and I suppose that's true. But it seems to me that the money on the Tour didn't start to get up where it is today until three younger players—Arnold Palmer, Jack Nicklaus, and Gary Player—came around. Maybe it takes a threesome to make golf grow. I don't know. We'll see if a couple of other young players, like Ernie Els and Justin Leonard, can step up and give Tiger Woods a run for the money to keep things exciting.

# ARNOLD PALMER

Arnold Palmer came along at just the right time. Arnold had a personality, a charm, and a style that fit with television. He played a huge role in creating a wider audience for professional golf. Arnold also had what it took to compete and win. People still love to watch Arnold. They relate to him, and he relates to them. He seems to get energy, strength, and confidence from golf galleries. Arnold wasn't a privileged kid. He grew up working hard, learning his trade from his father, Deacon Palmer, who was a pro in western Pennsylvania. Deacon demanded discipline from Arnold and made him recognize that it's the people who pay to watch him play who matter. You should treat them with respect and make it work for you rather than against you. So many young players today view the fans as either a distraction or even as a tedious drain on their energy. I firmly believe Arnold won many tournaments on the strength of his relationship with the gallery, with the force of "Arnie's Army."

Arnold's swing technique was always a little different. But he understood how to win the real battles. Deacon trained him well. He gave him the secret early in his life when he told him that "golf was the only game played from the neck up."

I think Jack Nicklaus in his prime was our best putter. Well, when Arnold was good, he was better than Jack! He was very bold. After knocking it five feet past the hole, he wouldn't think anything about it and just go up to it and knock it in. What did they say? "Charge, Arnie. Charge!"

I always said, boy oh boy, if Arnold had a great swing . . . His left elbow comes up through impact and he starts hooking the ball, and he's fought that hook his whole career. Of course, Arnold always swung that way. The record books don't notice where your elbow or anything else is, and we all know what a great champion Arnold has been. And just look at what his charisma and wonderful personality has done for golf.

But if he had had a better swing, there's no telling what he would have done. Arnold was like Tiger Woods; he wanted to kill everybody. That's the kind of competitor he was.

# GARY PLAYER

Maybe I should have spent more time playing over in South Africa because it might have helped my putting. I say that because like his countryman Bobby Locke, Gary Player was one heck of a good putter. Come to think of it, young Ernie Els and the Senior Tour player John Bland aren't too shabby with the flat stick either, and they're both from South Africa . . . but don't let me get too far afield.

Gary was always a good sound player. He was a great trap and wedge player, and he drove the ball straight. That's why he's won all those majors. I'll tell you something else. You can't meet a better guy than Gary Player.

Gary kept himself in better shape than anybody on the Tour. You could say he was like an alcoholic in his addiction to eating right, getting exercise, and keeping himself fit. He didn't smoke, and I've never seen him take a drink.

Gary would let his right foot step forward through impact, so it looked as if he were chasing his ball right down the fairway after he hit. It reminds me of one time when Lawson Little was playing Jim Ferrier. When Jim hit, his right foot went forward, then his left foot trailed. He would hit the ball, and the people would clap. Lawson said, "Jim, I don't know if they were applauding your good shot or your broad jump!" So you see, everybody's got his or her own way of doing it.

# JACK NICKLAUS

Jack Nicklaus was raw power with a great putting touch. He overpowered golf courses with his length and could hit shots, especially high, soft iron shots, that could make your mouth water. His achievements and his domination, especially of the majors, were stirring the public's interest in the grand old game.

Jack's concentration is legendary. Even when he was young he was able to focus in on what had to be done. When I won my first major championship, the gallery was clearly in favor of my opponent, Jim Turnesa. When Jack won his first major at the age of twenty-two, he played in a play-off against Arnold. Of course, at that time Arnold was The King. Beyond that, the championship was held at Oakmont Country Club in Pittsburgh, Pennsylvania, which was not far from Latrobe, where Arnie grew up.

Needless to say, the fans got very ugly. Arnie's Army was very vocal in favor of their guy, and more than once Palmer fans heckled Jack as he prepared to putt, saying, "Miss it, Fat Jack!"

Due to his great powers of concentration, Jack prevailed in the play-off, winning 71–74. After the play-off, Jack was asked if the crowd bothered him. Jack said, "Crowd? What crowd?"

More often than not, Jack was able to zone in and block out distractions—probably better than anyone in history. While I achieved this on occasion, I wish I hadn't let so many things bother me on others.

Another mental aspect I felt Jack had was fearlessness. Many golfers create such mental distortions and exaggerations that they can't perform because of their fears. Jack always seems to play a course without any fear at all.

Nicklaus once said that he did have fears like everyone else, but that he recognized them and faced them squarely. He would say to himself, "Okay, what are you afraid of? You're obviously playing well or you wouldn't be here. Go ahead, enjoy yourself. Play one shot at a time and meet the challenge!"

I can remember having this kind of talk with myself, and it sure helped. Besides, I always thought there were only three things to fear in golf: lightning, Ben Hogan, and a downhill putt!

Though I'm about thirty years Jack's senior, I went down to the wire with Nicklaus on a couple of occasions. One was way back during the Doral Open in Miami, where he beat me, and another was at Pebble Beach.

At Pebble, we got to the seventeenth hole and were right there together in the lead. You may recall that hole has a special meaning for Jack. During the 1972 U.S. Open, he hit the flagstick on seventeen with a one iron and the ball came to rest just a couple of inches away from the hole. Nicklaus went on to win that Open, and even he has said that may be the most memorable shot he ever hit.

Well, this is going back a few years before that, but it was the same hole. I'm not the first to say it, so I don't feel bad about mentioning that Nicklaus was never known to be a great wedge or sand player. Heck, he hit the ball on the green all the time anyway, so he didn't have to be. But the flag was cut on the green that day in such a tough spot that you'd be luckier than sin to get the ball near the hole. He hit it in the bunker, and I hit a low one iron into the trap as well. Since I was a good sand player, I figured I'd have a good chance against him. Wouldn't you know it, it was my ball that was buried! So much for planning ahead. On top of that, Nicklaus made a twenty-footer on the last hole.

Nicklaus was very strong and had that upright swing, a combination that made playing from the rough a lot easier for him than for a lot of guys. He'd pluck that thing out of there with no trouble at all. I might have seen some players I thought were better than Jack from tee to green, but part of that was because he would hit it in the rough occasionally since he hit it so long. But no one was better than Jack on the green. It's all won and lost there, anyway. If you don't believe me, go look in the record books under Jack Nicklaus's name.

# Hogan, Nelson, and Me Against Jack Nicklaus and the Modern Players

I don't think you can compare players from different eras, because so many things have changed. The courses today are different, they're in better condition, and they're longer. The equipment is different—the ball flies a lot farther, and shafts and heads are different. The players are different, too. Today, they have a lot of advantages we didn't have, such as advances in training, medicine, ease of travel, better accommodations, and other courtesies. The depth and quality of the fields today are much better.

If Hogan, Nelson, and I were in our absolute primes today, hitting the ball exactly the way we did in the forties and fifties, we would be very competitive. If Nicklaus was also in his prime today he would be the best of us. He was a long straight driver, and he was a great putter. That's a combination you rarely see. For a period of about fifteen years he was a great putter. It seemed like every time I turned on the TV he was holing a fourteen-footer. Nelson, Hogan, and I would have held our own. I thought we were all better shot makers than Nicklaus, but Nicklaus was longer in his prime and I thought he putted better over time.

In a way, the modern player doesn't have to be a great shot maker because of the way courses are designed and set up today. You don't have to fashion shots to fit holes so much anymore.

When we played, you could hit it down the middle 225 yards and that would do very nicely. If you hit it 225 nowadays, it seems as if you still have another 250 left. Well, with today's players, it's full blast, one speed—110 percent—like Tiger Woods and Greg Norman!

One thing I will say about today's players, they can go from wire to wire more so than when I played. In my day, the leader after the first day would say, "I can't do any better than that," and he'd go get drunk!

# TIGER CUB

About fifteen years ago, just past my seventieth birthday, I played two holes with a cute little six-year-old named Tiger Woods. You know what? He swung the club similar to the way he swings it today. I have to laugh a little, because that's what people have been telling me about my swing for years—it hasn't changed. A golf swing is like a personality—once it forms, it stays fundamentally the same. You could say it only gets better or worse. Tiger's has gotten better, as his banker would certainly agree.

I remember thinking after watching the youngster bat the ball around the golf course that day that he would amount to something if he stuck with it. It may sound funny, but I believe I could get away with making the same statement today. Even with a Masters victory and all those Tour wins under his twenty-one-year-old belt, I don't think any of us know just how good this young man is going to be.

# TIGER WOODS

I went to the Nissan Open (which was called the Los Angeles Open in my day) a few years ago and was asked to take a look at Tiger Woods, who was playing in his first professional tournament as an amateur. Of course, everyone knows Tiger Woods now, and he is breaking new ground every day. I think he was only sixteen years old at the time, and I rode out to watch him play the tenth hole (at the Riviera Country Club, site of my 1950 play-off victory over Ben Hogan in his celebrated return to the tour after his accident). The tenth is a little pitch-and-putt par four. Tiger had hit an iron in the left rough, missed the green—which is only about as big as my den— and made bogey. The next hole is a long par five, and Tiger hooked it left, pitched it back onto the fairway, and hit his third into the barranca. At that point, I thought maybe I shouldn't follow him in case it was making him self-conscious or making him press too hard.

A piece of advice I would give Tiger is to take great care of himself so that his young, strong body doesn't break down. He can have a long and successful career then. I am amazed at the speed he generates and the distances he hits the ball. Just as I would tell John Daly, there are lots of guys who can hit it three hundred plus yards. The woods are full of them.

I receive quite a few phone calls each week asking me my opinion of Tiger's swing. Some of the reporters have suggested that Tiger is breaking new ground, and some suggest that there are similarities to the way I did things. I see that he plays a power game and that he is much longer than other players. I do see a few similarities between us. He has that tremendous shoulder turn and uses his legs and hips well—things I think I did. If you look at pictures of me in my younger days and Tiger today, you will see both these things in our swings. At impact our hips are completely turned out of the way, showing that the downswing power first is generated by an athletic move into the left side and then rotated—hard! Both of us turned our shoulders more than one hundred degrees at the top of the backswing. His is a great swing, no doubt about it. I just think he goes at it more than the 85 percent I did, and that may cost him.

I like Tiger's swing, but I hope his coach doesn't shorten his backswing any more. Tiger's power is in his body just before impact, and if he shortens his backswing too much, his body won't have time to get set for the downswing and that can really spell trouble. His mental attitude, however, is as good as I have ever seen.

Tiger Woods, when the book is finally written, will have a chapter all his own. He has created more attention for golf than any other person in history. The sheer number of people who are now interested in golf from all segments of our society—young and old, black and white, male and female—is incredible.

Tiger has done more than raise the bar. It's not just that the standards of excellence have been lifted, it's the impact on the game and bringing people into it who may not have been in it before. Tiger is great for golf. I always wanted to play against the best players in the game. It made me more interested and more motivated when they showed up. If the impact that Tiger has is to bring better players and better athletes into the game, and if the present players raise their games up a notch or two, it will be a great development!

# TIGER, THE SYMBOL

I hope Tiger continues to do well. This is important, because he represents not only himself but African-Americans as well. I had seen how dreadfully some fans (and players) had treated my friend Charlie Sifford when he broke the racial barrier in golf. Charlie is a good man and deserved to be treated as a man and a good player. I was very happy to see that after his great Masters victory, Tiger thanked Charlie Sifford for doing some of the hard work and enduring some pretty bad treatment.

Charlie still plays well today and plays an occasional senior event. Charlie was famous for smoking a cigar while he swung. He had a good, simple swing, and his swing thought was the simplest ever: "Swing under your cigar." Man, could he hit it straight! About five or six years ago he led the Senior Tour in fairways hit with 85 percent.

There were other good black players in my day. Teddy Rhodes was one of the best. Later, Lee Elder and, much later, Calvin Peete would come along. And don't forget my pal, Joe Louis, the heavyweight champion. He did a lot to bring attention to the plight of the black athlete. He played in some Tour events, but he mostly teed it up on the old Negro Tour, which was like the old Negro baseball league. This was before the PGA changed its bylaws to allow black golfers to compete in PGA events. Joe wasn't as good as he thought and not in a class with Sifford and Rhodes and those fellows. He tried to compete with them. One time he was in a match with Rhodes and, on the eighteenth hole, turned to his caddie and asked, "How much to the hole?"

The caddie replied, "About a bogey and ten bucks to Mr. Ted."

## HOGAN'S SECRET

At one time Ben Hogan had such a long backswing that the shaft of his driver would point straight down at the ground. About the third round of a tournament, a Red Grange—number seventy-seven—might slip in there and the other players would go by Ben in bunches. Seventy-seven may look fine on a football jersey, but it's not too pretty on a pro's scorecard.

Ben changed his swing two different times. The first time, he was hitting hooks. Hooks, hooks, hooks . . . and not too high at that. Well, with those hard greens out there on the Tour, he couldn't hold them. So he turned around, shortened his swing and weakened his grip, started to cut the ball, and did his best work.

Ben said, "I have got something about the golf swing, and I will never, ever tell it to anybody." They started calling it something like "Hogan's Secret." I think even one of the magazines wrote about what it was, so I guess Ben wound up telling it to somebody, unless he gave out something else!

Ben would say to me, "Don't tell these other players anything, they don't appreciate it," and so on. I never felt that way and would help a guy out when I could.

Heck, Ben didn't have to keep it a secret anyway . . . you could see what it was. He started to keep or extend his right arm straight through the ball, which helped him keep the club head going straight down the line longer. That gave him a lot more control of his shots, so he started to get rid of that hook and his ball flight became a lot straighter. He began to play that famous fade.

Ben used to say he wanted to keep his right elbow tight against his right side through the ball. He'd talk about how he would wear out his sweater where his right elbow rubbed against his side down in the hitting area. I played with Hogan quite a bit, and I'd watch him practice hitting balls, so I knew exactly what his secret was: His arm was straight through the ball. Other people might disagree with me about this, but I'm sure that was his secret. That was what I saw.

You can't keep a secret in golf. The other guy is watching.

# MY SECRET

After telling people over and over again that what golf is all about is rhythm and timing, I'm not sure I can legitimately even call it a secret anymore. But that's what golf is: rhythm and timing. There. I've said it again!

When I say rhythm, I'm talking about music, not

some general notion about rhythm like the rhythm of the seasons or something like that.

Have you ever watched figure skaters? You see how when the music is turned on, they get right into the beat? I would love to play golf with music playing over a loudspeaker. That's where the rhythm and timing comes in—it's "one, two, three . . ." My swing feels as if it is slow going back and slow starting down, then gradually picks up speed until I get that pop! at impact. "One, two, *three* . . ." Something like that. When I'm playing well, I just feel—how did that old radio-show host put it? I just "swing and sway with Sammy Kaye."

The music you want to hear when you swing is something slow; a waltz is better than a fox trot. Of course, a lot of the younger people out there might not even know what a waltz is anymore. I don't think some of their music I hear today when I flick past those music channels with the TV remote control would work very well for golf.

# INFORMATION OVERLOAD

I think one of the biggest problems on the PGA Tour today is that players depend on too many other people. I have a great respect for teachers, but I think today's teachers tell players too much. They don't give them room to learn on their own. As soon as some of today's players hit a bad shot or two, they fall apart, and then they're on the practice tee and the coach is moving them this way and that.

I've said many times there's definitely such a thing as being "too much pro'd." I mean, you get overloaded with information. You get away from your fundamentals.

The best teacher you can ever have is yourself. In professional golf, you're out there all alone, except for your caddie, and you had better know how to correct things on your own.

I've always found that the best way to play is to think about your swing while you practice and then forget about it. Always try to have a blank mind while you are swinging during a round.

---

## Mark Steinbauer on Sam

---

I have tried to learn about golf and golf training by spending time with many of the world's best teachers, and I have learned very valuable information from each of them. I feel that Harvey Penick was the best teacher of all time, and when he was a young man he was quite a player. Harvey always used to say that after watching Sam Snead hit the ball he decided to become a teacher.

Sam Snead was known as Mr. Tempo to most people. I don't know of anyone who doesn't marvel at the longevity of his career. Sam had great motion, and because of that he was more of a swinger of the club than a hitter of the ball. I learned from Sam Snead that good motion will make up for a lot of sins. From what Harvey taught me and from the results Sam got, it emphasized to me the importance of keeping good tempo in the swing. When I have a student who is having trouble from being too mechanical or position-oriented, I like to use motion drills. After all, Sam, one of the best swingers of all times, aimed right of his target and swung his club to the left. Jeff Maggert also speaks frequently of his tempo, as if this is his main concern. To see the results these players get from emphasizing tempo serves as a great lesson to me.

---

# AIMING RIGHT

Most golfers have to be careful about their alignment. I never used much in the way of aids to help me, but I can remember hitting the ball cockeyed when I got out of alignment. At the 1949 Masters, I was on that wonderful practice ground and another player who saw I was struggling said, "Hey, Sam, do you know you're aiming over there in those trees?" I said, "You're kidding!" But, by golly, when I laid clubs down to check my alignment, I was aimed way to the right. I straightened my alignment back up and won the tournament.

For most of my career I aimed a little right and played a small draw. Sometimes I got lined up more and more right, and, before you knew it, it was more and more hook. I think we get into habits like this unconsciously and that's how fades turn into slices and draws into hooks.

Actually, I did come over the ball a wee bit, like Jones and some others. Everybody who's played the game has a little quirk in his aiming, and sometimes it causes bad shots.

I've watched Greg Norman a lot. He told me once that he likes to open his left foot—to flair it out a little in order to hit the ball farther. Under pressure, I think he has a tendency to let his body get going too fast so it gets out ahead of the ball, causing him to hit shots to the right of his target.

# TODAY'S PLAYERS AND TODAY'S TOUR

I watch golf on television, and I attend the Masters, the Legends of Golf, and a few other tournaments each year, and I try to keep up with what's happening in professional golf.

I am happy about the growth of the tours these days. The increases in the purses and the contributions to charity show how healthy the game is. I am not sure that the amount of money around is a totally good thing, however. I hear a few too many players saying they are playing just to make a good check or to have a high finish. That bothers me. I think a golfer ought to have his mind on trying to find a way to win—he ought to have a little fire in his belly. I don't think as many of today's players have that will to win that great champions seem to have.

Of the modern group of players, I enjoy watching Greg Norman. He has that presence, that flair, and I think he's the best player out there. I don't like how he shortened his swing recently. His swing of a few years ago was a very good one. It was more upright and not as behind him and flat in the backswing. I think he'll win several more majors. He's a good putter, and when he gets going he's unbeatable, unless he beats himself.

Nick Faldo has proven a lot over the last few years. I actually liked his old swing, too. It had good tempo, it flowed, and he hit the ball sweetly. I think he tinkers too much with his swing, but one thing is for sure, when the pressure is on he's a great competitor. He seems to trust himself more than any other player.

Among the other current players I really enjoy watching are Tom Watson, Phil Mickelson, Tom Lehman, Davis Love, and Justin Leonard. I was happy to see Tom Watson win at the Memorial in 1996. Tom's more of a veteran player and shot maker and, like me, has suffered through some of his own problems with putting. During the eighties, you could count on the ball dropping into the cup whenever he was on or near the green! I like to watch Mickelson because he has a graceful style, and, boy, can he putt! Leonard looks as if he has the whole package and won his first major, the '97 British Open, while Lehman had a great year in 1996 and looks to be maturing into a solid, multiple winner for years to come.

# THE FINISH OF A GOOD SWING

On a normal shot I come up into my finish and the club shaft is balanced between my ears, roughly perpendicular to my shoulders. A lot of amateurs don't pay much attention to a balanced finish, but I think it's important.

I helped young Davis Love with his finish position in 1995. I have known Davis since he was a little boy. His dad and I worked together in some *Golf Digest* schools. I played with him a few times when he was younger, but I don't remember being overwhelmed by his talent—as I am now. I'm glad he finally won a major!

Davis had a huge arc—very high hands in the backswing. I remember watching him win the tournament at New Orleans to qualify for the Masters. He hooked a seven iron into the trap on the left on seventeen and a six iron into the trap on the left at eighteen.

At Augusta the next week I told Davis that he was aimed right and was doing what we call corking off, cutting off the swing in the downswing. Davis said, "Well, thank you, Sam." By keeping his arc the same on both sides of the ball and having an inside attack and a balanced finish, Davis was able to be more constant, almost winning the 1995 Masters.

You should be able to hold your balanced finish and pose just a bit.

# THREE CONTEMPORARY SWINGS

When you get down to it, it's not that hard to tell a good swing from a bad swing. What you want to look for is how a player's swing stays smooth through the ball. Watch Steve Elkington. You wouldn't want a better swing. Through the ball he's well under control and very smooth. But sometimes he stays back on his right foot a little longer than most people.

Now, Mark O'Meara is another player today with an awfully good swing. It's simple, and he keeps it right on the plane. But I don't give a damn how well a player swings, he had better be a good putter, and Mark O'Meara is one of the better putters on the Tour. He's even better when it gets right down to the real nitty-gritty and he's facing a putt that really counts.

Nick Faldo also has pretty much of a simple swing, and he doesn't look as if he labors much with it. That's the swing itself I'm talking about. Before he hits the ball, he fools around, pulls up his pants, grips the club two or three times, walks up to the ball, fiddles around. And I think to myself, Gosh, I don't see how he can concentrate, but, evidently, he does.

# UNCLE SAM

My brother Jesse's son, my nephew Jesse Carlyle, is better known as J. C. Snead. J.C. now plays regularly on the Senior Tour after having had a solid career, with eight wins on the regular Tour. Since joining the Senior Tour, J.C. comes home with a problem and says, "Hey, Unky, I want you to watch me hit a few." Well, I straighten him out in ten minutes.

J.C. has gotten himself in a situation now where he's not playing as well as he has in the past. I wish he'd come home for a week so I could straighten him back out.

This is the way it is out there, even on the Senior Tour. There's so many guys who have tutors and teachers and everything else. If you ask five different teaching pros something, they'll give you five different answers. I've never seen anything like it in my life. One guy says keep your head still. The other guy says turn your head when you make a backswing. Another says make sure you keep your left heel on the ground. J.C.'s listening to too many people, and it has got him so confused he doesn't know whether he's afoot or on horseback. You can't tell a guy but one thing at a time.

J.C. has had his share of problems with his putting, too. I guess it runs in the family. If there's a good putter among us Sneads, well, I don't know of him.

## THE NEW GURU

I get a call once in a while from Tour players who would like me to help them out with their swings. My son Jackie likes to talk about how recently in

Augusta at the Masters, Ian Woosnam, Seve Balles-
teros, Nick Faldo, and some others were standing
around with me on the clubhouse porch at the top
of old Magnolia Lane on Tuesday night after the
Champions Dinner. They were shadow swinging
without a club and asking me what I thought about
this or that in their technique. Well, that was a lot of
fun.

Vijay Singh called not long ago and asked if I
would look at his swing, so we set up a lesson for
him at the Players' Championship in Jacksonville.
Now, Vijay told me that he modeled his swing after
mine. Heck, I might go ahead and model my swing
after his if I were a young player on the Tour today.
But I told him I would take a look.

Vijay was coming up and out of his shot a little
early, which made him hit it a bit thin. I had him put
his four iron right down there behind the ball at
address and asked him to shut his eyes and get a
good visual image of that iron sitting behind the ball.
Then I told him to think only about returning that
four iron to that same visual image he had of it sitting there behind the ball during the takeaway. That
was the trick that did it, because it kept him there
through the ball long enough to make more solid
contact. If he wanted to look up after that, it was all
right, because he had already hit the ball by then.
Before you knew it, he was hitting all of his shots
rock-solid again.

Then Ernie Els called and asked if I would play with him in the par three tournament at the '97 Masters. We did, with his countryman from South Africa, Gary Player, rounding out our group. Boy, what a good swing young Ernie has!

Well, afterward, I received the nicest letter from him that you could ever want to get. He thanked me for playing with him in the par three and said how he had read all of my books and was looking forward to buying my new instruction video. Now, that got Jackie and me to thinking.

Jackie said that he thought a lot of those players out on the Tour would love to have me look at them hitting balls and help them out if I could. He just wondered whether they felt awkward or uncomfortable about asking me. Well, what does my good friend Gary Player say? "Rest is rust." As I said, I enjoy working with the boys. What Jackie and I are thinking about doing is putting together a letter and distributing it to the fellas on the PGA and Senior tours saying I'm inviting them to give me a call and come see me at the Greenbrier if they think they need a little help. All they have to do is get themselves down here and pay for their stay. I won't charge them for the lessons.

What the heck, I might even become one of those . . . what do they call them . . . "teaching gurus"? . . . before too long!

# COST-OF-LIVING INCREASE

What can you say about the money out there on the Tour these days? Tiger Woods has won $2 million in less than one calendar year. Astronomical! Some people, however, say that the professional golfer doesn't make enough when compared with the top players in other sports, and I have to admit there's something to that. A golfer has to win every cent he makes, and golfers don't have a team behind them picking up the slack when they're a little off their game or an organization paying their expenses—first class, at that! So here I am defending golfers and the big money they make.

When the professional golf tour started, before I even thought about playing out there, the players put up their own money to create the prize purses for each tournament. As I've said for the last fifty-one years, it cost me $2,000 to go play in the British Open, and I got $600 for winning it. When I beat Hogan at the

Masters in a play-off in 1954, I got $3,400, including the eighteen-hole play-off. No overtime!

I won a thousand for winning the first Crosby. The biggest check I ever got for winning the Miami Open, which I won six times, was $750, and you had to put yourself up in Miami for a week.

People ask if I get angry about this discrepancy in prize money. Well, times change and it was cheaper to live then. I could stay down there in Miami at a hotel for a dollar a night. Even so, why get angry? It's "Too bad, old buddy, we can't help you there." What gets to me just a little bit is that some players today don't think about who paved the road for them. But that's just the way things are.

## MATCH-PLAY MEMORIES

Today, with the exception of the Ryder Cup, almost all of the Tour's events are medal or stroke play, not match play. Many of my wins, including all of my three PGA Championships, were match play. Actually, I enjoyed match play more than I did medal play, because you only had one guy to contend with, one guy at a time, that is.

I watched the guys I had to contend with very closely. I could tell you all of their mannerisms. I could even look at a pair of shoes lying in the locker room and tell you who they belonged to. I tried to know my opponent inside out.

If a guy suddenly waggles three times instead of two, he's changing his mannerisms. Invariably, maybe 95 percent of the time after that, the guy would hit a bad shot, and I'd say to myself, "I gotcha now!"

I'm not so sure, looking back, that I was aware my opponents were paying attention to my mannerisms at the same time for the same reason.

I like match play, but I'll tell you one reason why we don't see more of it today. Let's look at the old format for the PGA Championship. If it comes down to two guys you never heard of in the final match, nobody will show up to watch them, right? So the PGA thought, Well, hey, we're losing a lot of money doing this. Let's have four days of medal play where most of the top guys will be playing four straight days. In match play, if you had a bad selection for the finish, the whole thing was out the window.

Television, with the exception of the Ryder Cup, only spelled more trouble for match play. With TV, even if you have two top players in the final match of a tournament, their match may come to a conclusion early, say, on the twelfth hole. Well, what do you do with the rest of the telecast time? So it doesn't look good for the future of match play on the Tour. Though I like it, I agree with all the reasons I just mentioned as to why we don't see much of it anymore. Everything has to change with the times.

# AUGUSTA PERENNIAL

For the past couple of years, Gene Sarazen, Byron Nelson, and I hit ceremonial drives off the first tee at Augusta National to get the Masters started. It's a lot of fun seeing all the guys again, and the fans seem to love it. They line that first fairway three deep at eight o'clock on Thursday morning. It's something I've come to really look forward to.

Well, last year, when I walked up on the tee, Joe Phillips from Wilson handed me a brand-new driver.

It was kind of a scary thing, though I got the shot off all right. I don't know who was happier about that, Joe Phillips, Wilson, or me.

## MY BUSINESSES TODAY

I've got some businesses with my son Jackie and my daughter-in-law Ann. I'm most proud of my Sam Snead's Taverns. With golf, nostalgia, sports memorabilia, and theme restaurants being so popular, this is a natural. Look at Don Shula's steakhouses in Florida and Michael Jordan's restaurant in Chicago, for instance, not to mention all the Hard Rock Cafes, Planet Hollywoods, and Harley-Davidson Cafes. Sam Snead's Taverns serve good food and drink in an atmosphere that is virtually a Sam Snead museum! In a Sam Snead Tavern, with its rich wood interiors and trophy cases filled with my old equipment, trophies, and photos, it's almost like being in a fancy clubhouse. And there's even a line of shirts and hats you can buy with the straw hat and instantly recognizable golf club logo. The success of the first five taverns, in Orlando; the Greenbrier; Hot Springs, Virginia; Myrtle Beach; and Atlanta, will determine whether or not they spread overseas or to their natural locations—on site at golf courses around the country.

Another business I've got going is golf clothes. When I was young, I was always known as one of the snappiest dressers on the golf course. I even got an award for it one year! Players like Greg Norman and Payne Stewart have taken their interest in clothes beyond the links and into the pro shops and department stores around America. With what fashion types call the "retro look" being in now, the classic clothing styles I wore in the 1940s and '50s should have great sales appeal. Look how Bobby Jones's name has bounced back with lines of clothes, balls, and clubs.

As for equipment, my company, Sam Snead Enterprises, is currently negotiating with Wilson to come out with a line of Sam Snead Senior oversized clubs. Right now, Wilson does not offer a line of clubs specifically for seniors, as Cobra and some other manufacturers do.

# ROCKS OF AGES

When you get to be my age, you tend to look back at the things you've done, your achievements as well as your mistakes, and ask yourself how you measured up to the standard you set for yourself. I think I've done pretty well.

To me, what has mattered most is a personal religion. I guess, though I can't be sure, that this grew out of an awareness of the importance of doing things the right way, upholding standards, having certain thoughts and feelings, and treating others well. I can say that the way I have approached my golf career has been consistent with those standards. I try to be a man of my word and let my actions speak for themselves.

Although my reputation was one of being miserly and overly concerned with money, I don't feel this reputation fit the man. I certainly knew and respected the value of a dollar. I always lived modestly—just as I do today. I have never been interested in having material things. The stories that Bob Hope used to tell about my having buried my money in tomato cans in my backyard were all good fun. But that's *all* they were, just good fun.

When I was asked if I made enough money after a victory on tour, I would always say, "How much is enough?" Growing up the way I did, you wanted to be self-sufficient, to be prepared for anything.

My second son, Terry, is retarded. When he was born, I worried a lot about him, and I set up a trust fund to take care of the inevitable bills, medical and otherwise, that would pile up.

In Ashwood and Hot Springs, there are a number of little churches where the people of our region worship. I support their good work. One early memory I have is of hitting a rock through the Methodist Church window and beating a fast retreat into the woods before anyone discovered who the devil could be so careless. Much later, I bought and donated a pipe organ for the Methodist Church, as I would do for a couple of other churches. The gifts were penance for the sins of my youth. Maybe God has forgiven me now. I hope so.

Another charitable cause that touches my heart is a college scholarship fund for Appalachian kids who have talent but might not be able to attend college because their parents can't afford it. There are still so many people in this region who can barely make ends meet. I have had the opportunity to use some of the gifts I've been given, and I want to see other kids have that opportunity as well. I also have a charity golf tournament in Orlando every year that benefits children.

My old caddie at the Greenbrier, Curtis Griffith, worked hard for me. I tried to take care of him and his family whenever I could. I bought him a car, a house, and other things that would make life easier for him. When his health failed and he couldn't work anymore, I would send groceries to his house.

When Freddy Martin, who first hired me at the Greenbrier, retired, I gave him and his wife a new car. He was *always* so kind and supportive of me.

Yes, I knew about not having and I didn't want people close to me to go without. Christmas was never a very big celebration to me as a child, and I can remember the feeling even today. Our presents were sometimes found under our plates. Usually it was a pair of socks, maybe two or three nickels. The biggest Christmas present I ever got was a sled that Dad had built.

# MY PLAY TODAY

At eighty-five, I still love this game, and I'm always working at it. I spend my winters in Fort Pierce, Florida, and live at the Meadowood Country Club; next I go to Augusta for the Masters, then head north for Hot Springs until winter sets in again. I still practice every day. When I'm home in Hot Springs, I get Meister—my golden retriever—and go down in my golf cart to the practice area at the Lower Cascades. I don't hit as many balls as I did in my prime, which was about five hundred a day. I would start with the wedge, then hit my seven iron, my five iron, the one or two iron, and finish up with my three wood and driver. Creamy Carolan, my personal caddie, would shag for me. Then I would go to the putting green.

Now I follow the same routine, but I hit only two hundred balls and I shag them myself. Meanwhile, Meister splashes around in the mountain creeks, looking for lost balls. He usually finds quite a few. I play about three times a week, sometimes more, sometimes less. And I find that if I want to hit a drive three hundred yards, I've got to go downhill and hit a few rocks and cart paths.

My health is still good. I've got some little problems—my left shoulder hasn't been right since that car accident. I've had a heart skip ever since I can remember, but I don't worry about it. My right eye is getting worse—I have a wrinkled retina, the ophthalmologist tells me. I can't see much out of it, so my depth perception is poor.

I still do my exercises—one hundred sit-ups in the morning and another hundred in the evening as well as forearm and biceps curls—and I have good eating habits. I eat red meat in moderation, with a lot of salads and green leafy vegetables. I also take minerals and vitamins. I get a kick out of telling the youngsters I meet to punch me in my midsection, as my muscles are still pretty strong and firm.

# APPENDIX

SAM SNEAD'S NOTABLE ACHIEVEMENTS

Sam Snead was declared the number-one-ranked golfer of all time by the PGA Tour Points System.

- Player of the Year, 1949
- 1938, 1949, 1950, 1955 Vardon Trophy Winner
- Holds world record for lowest average of the Vardon Trophy—69.23 for ninety-six rounds, 1950
- Named to Ryder Cup Teams in 1937, 1939 (no tournament), 1941 (no tournament), 1947, 1949, 1951, 1953, 1955, 1959. Sam was playing captain in 1953 and 1959. He was the nonplaying captain in 1969.
- 1960 and 1961 World Cup teams
- 1949, 1952, 1954 Masters winner
- 1946 British Open winner
- 1942, 1949, 1951 PGA Championship winner
- Member of the PGA and World Golf Halls of Fame, the Helms Hall of Fame, the Virginia Hall of Fame, and the West Virginia Hall of Fame
- 1949 and 1950 PGA leading money winner
- Sam shot a world record 59 in a USGA-sanctioned golf tournament, the 1959 Greenbrier Open

- Sam has finished in first place 185 times.
- Sam has finished in second place sixty-three times.
- Sam has finished in third place fifty-four times.
- Sam has finished in the Top 10 358 times and in the Top 25 473 times.
- Sam has had a hole in one with every club in the bag except the putter.
- Sam has had thirty-seven holes in one and four double eagles.
- Sam has set 164 course records.
- If Sam had shot 69 in the last round, he would have won nine U.S. Opens.
- Sam has won tournaments in six decades!
- Sam won the Greater Greensboro Open for the first time in 1938 and for the eighth time in 1965—a span of twenty-seven years, which is still the record.
- At the age of seventy-four, Sam shot 60 on the Lower Cascade's Golf Course in Hot Springs, Virginia, tying J. C. Snead's record.

SAM SNEAD'S FAMOUS FIRSTS

- Won the first Bing Crosby Tournament, 1937
- First recipient of the green jacket for winning the Masters, 1949
- Last double-digit winner on tour, with eleven victories, 1950
- Oldest winner on the PGA Tour. Won the 1965 Greater Greensboro Open at the age of fifty-two years, ten months, and eight days.
- Won the first Legends of Golf, 1978

· First player to shoot his age in a PGA Tour event. At age sixty-seven, Sam shot a 67 in the second round of the Quad Cities Open and a 66 in the final round, 1979.

SAM SNEAD'S TOURNAMENT VICTORIES

1936   West Virginia PGA, West Virginia Open, West Virginia Closed Professional, Virginia Closed Professional

1937   West Virginia Open, Bing Crosby Tournament, Miami Open, Nassau Open, Oakland Open, St. Paul Open

1938   Bing Crosby Tournament, Canadian Open, Chicago Open, Goodall Round Robin, Greensboro Open, Inverness Four-Ball, Westchester 108-Hole Open, White Sulphur Springs Open, St. Paul Open, Greenbrier Open, West Virginia Open, West Virginia PGA

1939   Miami Biltmore Four-Ball, Miami Open, Ontario Open, St. Petersburg Open

1940   Anthracite Open, Canadian Open, Inverness Four-Ball, Ontario Open

1941   Bing Crosby Tournament, Canadian Open, Henry Hurst Invitational, North-South Open, Rochester Times Union Open, St. Augustine Pro-Am, St. Petersburg Open

1942   Córdoba Open, PGA Championship, St. Augustine Pro-Am Championship, St. Petersburg Open

1943   Military Service—U.S. Navy during World War II

1944   Portland Open, Richmond Open, Middle Atlantic Open

1945  Dallas Open, Gulfport Open, Jacksonville Open, Los Angeles Open, Pensacola Open, Tulsa Open, Eleventh Naval Open—San Diego

1946  British Open, Greensboro Open, Jacksonville Open, Miami Open, Virginia Open, World Championship, War Bond Open

1947  Bing Crosby Pro-Am

1948  Seminole Pro-Am, Texas Open, Havana Invitational, Havana Pro-Am, West Virginia Open, West Virginia PGA

1949  Dapper Dan Open, Greensboro Open, Masters, PGA Championship, Washington Star Open, Western Open, Capitol City, Decatur Open, National Celebrities, West Virginia PGA, West Virginia Open

1950  Bing Crosby Pro-Am, Colonial National Invitational, Greensboro Open, Inverness Four-Ball, Los Angeles Open, Miami Beach Open, Miami Open, North-South Open, Reading Open, Texas Open, Western Open, Quarter Century Open

1951  Miami Open, PGA Championship, Greenbrier Open, Inverness Round Robin, Quarter Century Open

1952  All-American Open, Eastern Open, Greenbrier Pro-Am, Inverness Four-Ball, Julius Boros Open, Masters, Palm Beach Round Robin, Canadian Open, West Virginia Open, Greenbrier Festival, Seminole Pro-Am, Mid-South Open—Pinehurst

1953  Baton Rouge Open, Greenbrier Pro-Am, Texas Open, Greenbrier Festival, Orlando Two-Ball, Scranton (Pennsylvania) Open

| 1954 | Masters, Palm Beach Round Robin, Panama Open, Los Angeles Mixed with Babe Didrikson Zaharias, La Gorce Individual |
|------|------|
| 1955 | Greensboro Open, Insurance City Open, Miami Beach Open, Miami Open, Palm Beach Round Robin, Hartford Open, Bayshore Individual |
| 1956 | Greensboro Open, Boca Raton Open, San Diego Open |
| 1957 | Dallas Open, Palm Beach Round Robin, West Virginia Open, George Mays World Open |
| 1958 | Dallas Open, Greenbrier Invitational, Virginia Open, West Virginia Open, West Virginia PGA, Normandi Isle Open |
| 1959 | Sam Snead Festival, West Virginia PGA, George Mays All-American Open |
| 1960 | DeSoto Open, Greensboro Open, Hccks Open, Quarter Century Open |
| 1961 | Sam Snead Festival, Tournament of Champions, West Virginia Open |
| 1962 | Palm Beach Round Robin, West Virginia PGA |
| 1963 | West Virginia PGA |
| 1964 | Haig & Haig Scotch Mixed Foursome, PGA Seniors Championship, World Seniors Championship |
| 1965 | Greensboro Open—Sam became the oldest winner on the PGA Tour when he won the Greensboro, and still holds this title, PGA Seniors Championship, Haig & Haig Scotch Mixed Foursome, World Seniors Championship, West Virginia PGA |
| 1966 | Sam Snead/Greenbrier Festival, West Virginia PGA, West Virginia Open |

1967  PGA Seniors Championship, West Virginia PGA, West Virginia Open
1968  West Virginia Open
1969  El Dorado Professional Member
1970  PGA Seniors Championship, West Virginia PGA, Greenbrier Open, World Seniors Championship
1971  West Virginia Open, PGA Club Professional Championship
1972  PGA Seniors Championship, World Seniors Championship, Los Angeles Senior Championship, West Virginia Open
1973  PGA Seniors Championship, World Seniors Championship, CBS Golf Classic with Gardner Dickinson, Newport Seniors Championship, West Virginia Open
1978  Legends of Golf
1980  *Golf Digest* Commemorative
1982  Legends of Golf with Don January
1983  Legends of Golf with Gardner Dickson

# ABOUT THE AUTHORS

SAM SNEAD is the winningest golfer of all time, with 185 professional victories, and has coauthored twelve previous books.

FRAN PIROZZOLO, PH.D., is a well-known human-performance coach for many world-class athletes and the team psychologist for the New York Yankees. Fran, who works with many of the world's top golfers, recently coauthored *The Mental Pocket Companion*. He is a member of the teaching staff at the Doral Golf Learning Center in Miami. Fran was the Chief of Neuro-psychology Service at Baylor College of Medicine in Houston from 1981 to 1997.

JIM MCLEAN is the Director of the Jim McLean Golf Learning Center at Miami's Doral Country Club and Director of Instruction for KSL Properties. A former Tour player, PGA Teacher of the Year in 1994, and coach to many of the Tour's best players, Jim has published numerous golf books, including *The Eight-Step Swing, The Putter's Pocket Companion* with Fran Pirozzolo, and *Golf Digest's Book of Drills,* and has done instructional television and home videos, including the video *Sam Snead: A Swing for a Lifetime,* released by the Golf Channel in 1997.

# LARGE PRINT EDITIONS

## Look for these at your local bookstore

American Heart Association, *American Heart Association
        Cookbook, 5th Edition* (abridged)
Lauren Bacall, *Now* (paper)
Dave Barry, *Dave Barry Is Not Making This Up* (paper)
Peter Benchley, *White Shark* (paper)
John Berendt, *Midnight in the Garden of Good and Evil*
        (paper)
Barbara Taylor Bradford, *Angel* (paper)
Barbara Taylor Bradford, *Remember*
Marlon Brando with Robert Lindsey, *Brando:
        Songs My Mother Taught Me* (paper)
Leo Buscaglia, Ph.D., *Born for Love*
Joe Claro, editor, *The Random House Large Print Book
        of Jokes and Anecdotes* (paper)
Michael Crichton, *Disclosure* (paper)
Michael Crichton, *The Lost World* (paper)
Michael Crichton, *Rising Sun*
E. L. Doctorow, *The Waterworks* (paper)
Dominick Dunne, *A Season in Purgatory*
Fannie Flagg, *Daisy Fay and the Miracle Man* (paper)
Fannie Flagg, *Fried Green Tomatoes at the
        Whistle Stop Cafe* (paper)
Ken Follett, *A Place Called Freedom* (paper)
Robert Fulghum, *From Beginning to End: The Rituals of
        Our Lives*
Robert Fulghum, *It Was on Fire When I Lay Down
        on It* (hardcover and paper)
Robert Fulghum, *Maybe (Maybe Not): Second Thoughts
        from a Secret Life*
Robert Fulghum, *Uh-Oh*

(continued)

Gabriel García Márquez, *Of Love and Other Demons*
     (paper)
Martha Grimes, *The End of the Pier*
Martha Grimes, *The Horse You Came In On* (paper)
Martha Grimes, *Rainbow's End* (paper)
David Halberstam, *The Fifties* (2 volumes, paper)
Katharine Hepburn, *Me* (hardcover and paper)
P. D. James, *The Children of Men*
P. D. James, *Original Sin* (paper)
Pope John Paul II, *Crossing the Threshold of Hope*
Pope John Paul II, *The Gospel of Life* (paper)
Dean Koontz, *Dark Rivers of the Heart* (paper)
Dean Koontz, *Icebound*
Judith Krantz, *Dazzle*
Judith Krantz, *Lovers* (paper)
Judith Krantz, *Scruples Two*
John le Carré, *Our Game* (paper)
John le Carré, *The Secret Pilgrim*
Anne Morrow Lindbergh, *Gift from the Sea*
Cormac McCarthy, *The Crossing* (paper)
Audrey Meadows with Joe Daley, *Love, Alice* (paper)
James A. Michener, *Mexico* (paper)
James A. Michener, *Miracle in Seville* (paper)
James A. Michener, *Recessional* (paper)
James A. Michener, *The World Is My Home* (paper)
Sherwin B. Nuland, *How We Die* (paper)
Richard North Patterson, *Degree of Guilt*
Richard North Patterson, *Eyes of a Child* (paper)
Luciano Pavarotti and William Wright, *Pavarotti: My
     World* (paper)
Louis Phillips, editor, *The Random House Large Print
     Treasury of Best-Loved Poems*
Colin Powell with Joseph E. Persico, *My American
     Journey* (paper)